POETRY CO♪

GREAT MINDS

Your World...Your Future...YOUR WORDS

From Yorkshire & Lincolnshire
Edited by Jessica Woodbridge

 Young**Writers**
First published in Great Britain in 2005 by:
Young Writers
Remus House
Coltsfoot Drive
Peterborough
PE2 9JX
Telephone: 01733 890066
Website: www.youngwriters.co.uk

SB ISBN 1 84602 082 4

Foreword

This year, the Young Writers' 'Great Minds' competition proudly presents a showcase of the best poetic talent selected from over 40,000 up-and-coming writers nationwide.

Young Writers was established in 1991 to promote the reading and writing of poetry within schools and to the youth of today. Our books nurture and inspire confidence in the ability of young writers and provide a snapshot of poems written in schools and at home by budding poets of the future.

The thought, effort, imagination and hard work put into each poem impressed us all and the task of selecting poems was a difficult but nevertheless enjoyable experience.

We hope you are as pleased as we are with the final selection and that you and your family continue to be entertained with *Great Minds From Yorkshire & Lincolnshire* for many years to come.

Contents

Ramandeep Kaur (16)   1
Taranom Movahedi (12)   1

Caistor Yarborough School, Caistor
Jake Robinson-Steer (13)   2
Alex Jewitt (13)   3
Emily Tramaseur (13)   3
Sarah Shepherdson (13)   4
Chloe Tatam (13)   4
Joe Thompson (13)   5
Leona Brown (13)   5

Casterton Community College, Great Casterton
Laura Mitchell (11)   6
Sarah Webb (11)   6
Joseph Dulieu (11)   7
Thomas Birks (11)   7
Jake Loomes (11)   8
Nick Cunnington (11)   8
Daniel Wright (11)   9
Chelsea Cantwell (11)   9
Holly Duerden (11)   10
Emma Rice (11)   11
Charlotte Francis (11)   12
Charmaine Benton (11)   12
Emma Ward (12)   13
Ben Lewis (12)   13
Jake Walton (12)   14
Kate Billson (12)   14
Zoë Sargeant (12)   15
Amelia Shippey (11)   15
Katie Youngs (12)   16
Brydon Frith (12)   16
Jessica Blaes (12)   17
Tom Gregg (11)   17
Jessie Harris (11)   18
Bryony Smithers (11)   18
Carrie Enright (12)   19
Thomas Duffin (11)   19

Ben McClarnon (11)	20
Emily Rowbotham (11)	20
Sam Swann (12)	21
Jamie Rowlatt (12)	21
Sarah-Mae Yardley (11)	22
Jade Tebbutt (11)	22
Jacob McClarnon (11)	23
Sam Dobbs (12)	23
Jordan Holland (12)	24
Heather McClelland (11)	24
Gemma Sinfield (11)	25
Rosanna Williams (11)	25
Luke Fox (12)	26
Amber Buckley (11)	26
Louise Mossom (11)	27
Sam Bacon (11)	27
Thomas Kellett (11)	28
Rosie Barker (12)	28
Adam Purcell (11)	29
Megan Hooper (11)	29
Debra Czornookyj (11)	30
Chloe Berry (11)	30
Jacqui Pretlove (11)	30

Dixons City Technology College, Bradford

Ashraf Ebrahim (17)	31
Kamal Hussain (18)	31
Emma Parfitt (13)	32
Katie Sutcliffe (17)	33
Richard Bartlett (11)	34
Jonathan Rainer (12)	35
Aaron Newland (14)	36
Mohammed Anis (11)	37
Sumera Kauser (17)	38
Vaishali Mistry (12)	38

John Leggott College, Scunthorpe

Antony Lifsey (17)	39
Devon Warner (17)	40
Gina Davies (17)	41
Danielle Sempers (18)	42

Sarah Stevenson (16)   43
Jacky Wong (18)   44
Scott Fowler (16)   45

Monks' Dyke Technology College, Louth
James Newcome (16)   46

Queen Elizabeth's Grammar School, Horncastle
Catherine Watts (16)   47

Queen Elizabeth's High School, Gainsborough
Lorna Turner (12)   48
Dominic Powell (12)   48
Darcy Martin (12)   49
Hannah Balfour (11)   49
Chloe Smith (11)   50
Holly Southward (11)   51
Kalita Offer (12)   52
Holly Constable (11)   52
Jordan Tennant (11)   53
Mark Picken (11)   53
Luke Martin (12)   54
Danielle Wood (11)   55
Savannah Bowles (11)   56
Lewis Hancock (12)   56
Danielle Smith (11)   57
Emma Goodson (11)   57
Madison Devine (11)   58
Tom Fenwick (11)   59
Gemma Burns (11)   60
Ross Burnett (11)   60
Rebecca Gray (11)   61
Matthew Lawson (11)   61
Andrew McPheat (11)   62

St Bede's Catholic Grammar School, Bradford
Daniel O'Shea (13)   62
Joseph Buchaldzin (13)   63
Ashley McNulty (12)   63
Nathan O'Shea (12)   64

Faizhan Hussain (12)	64
Colum Sheridan-Small (12)	65
Jack Tidswell (12)	65
Usman Sarwar (12)	66
Christopher Riley (12)	67
Mark Furniss (12)	67
Luke Whitehead (12)	68
Toby Romano (12)	68
Jordan Watt (12)	69
Daniel Lowe (13)	69
Jacob Muff (13)	70
Christopher Hopwood (12)	70
Luke Jawnyj (13)	71
Jordan Lightowler (14)	71
Alex Blaikie (13)	72
David Rossiter (13)	72
Alex Machen (13)	73
James Le Blanc (13)	73
Isaac McGladdery (13)	74
Howard Usher (13)	75
Dominic Makohon-Keogh (13)	76
Thomas Crowley (13)	76
Christopher Polechonski (13)	77
Adam Cooke (13)	77
Ryan Newton (13)	78
Jamie Flinn (13)	79
Ryan Ingham (15)	80
Edward Isaac (13)	80
Joseph Begaj (14)	81
Jack Tallant (13)	81
Daniel Murgatroyd (14)	82
Leon Flerin (13)	83
Adam Glennon (13)	84
Matthias Chizalema (13)	84
Toby Sullivan (13)	85
Chris Jones (13)	85
Francis Barrett (13)	86
Jason Helstrip (13)	87
Ryan Buckroyd (13)	88
Jason Stockton (14)	89
Reece Thomas (13)	90
Myles Nesbitt (13)	90

Antony Cooper (15)	91
Stephen Harrison (13)	91
Chris Mitchell (13)	91
Matthew Riley (13)	92

The George Farmer Technology College, Holbeach

Paul Bennett (14)	92
Laura Goldsmith (14)	93
Rayner Coole (14)	93
Melany Clark (15)	94
Amy Wilson (14)	95
Kirsty Newby (14)	96
Josh Mann (14)	96
Steven Wetherell (14)	97
Sarah Thwaites (14)	97
Natasha Frolich (14)	98
Clementine Cousins (14)	98
Zoie Crowley (14)	99
Andy Dunham (14)	99
Beth Davis (14)	100
Naomi Stephens (14)	101
Jackie Cooke (15)	102
Laura Ashton (14)	102
Sean Gabriel (12)	103
Sam Collins (14)	103
Nicholas Mackelden (13)	104
Emma Frost (14)	104
Daniel Stanton (15)	105
Amber Rippin (14)	105
Danielle Coe (15)	106
Natalie Fensom (14)	106
Jodie Brogan (14)	107
Rhea Frederick (13)	107
Mandy Warren (15)	108
Kayleigh Brownsword (13)	108
Nicola Bullock (15)	109
Darren Taylor (15)	109
Duncan Cooke (14)	110
José Johnson (15)	110
Emma Inglis (14)	111
Stacey Doades (15)	111

Lindsay Graham (14)   112
Ben Flowers (14)   112
Kyle Rackham (14)   113
Adam Stacey (14)   113
Lee Lashmar (14)   114
Edward Carfrae (14)   115
Chamise Nocera (14)   116
Joanne Bradley (13)   116
Luke Hull (14)   117
Scott Goodale (13)   117
Daniel Rulewski (14)   118
Ricky Bramley (14)   118
Daniel Taylor (14)   119
Mark Wright (14)   119
Matt O'Leary (12)   120
Douglas Mitchell (14)   121
Emma Tierney (13)   122
Rachel Kirk (13)   122
Lucia Harness (13)   123
Francesca Fowler (13)   123
Laura Pearl (14)   124
Philip Teague (13)   124
Joshua Wells (13)   125
James Waters (13)   125
Ella Berrie (13)   126
Karl Barfoot (13)   126
Jack Putterill (13)   126
Ricky Crane (12)   127
Brendan Strowlger (13)   127
Cameron Flowers (13)   127
Kevin Hall (13)   128
Michelle Cook (13)   128
William Chenery (13)   129
Charlotte Bacon (12)   129
Charlotte Booth (12)   130
Jade Wells (12)   130
Sam Spencer (12)   131
Laura Thompson (12)   131
Leanne Frith-Anderson (12)   132
Daniel Meadows (12)   132
Craig Cumberworth (12)   133
Adam Smith (12)   133

Barbara Bearman (11)   134
Jack Robinson (12)   134
Zac Rowlett (12)   135
Sam Feetham (12)   135
AJ O'Connor (11)   136
Gemma Whincup (11)   136
Allan Taylor (12)   137
Holly Scott (11)   137
Holly Davis (11)   138
Jodie Wells (11)   139
Zoe Yorke (11)   139
Sian Hardy-Usher (11)   140
Ryan Isaacs (11)   140
Ben Brunton (11)   141
Emma Woods (11)   141
Chelsey Johnson (11)   142
Jack Beavis (12)   142

The Robert Manning Technology College, Bourne
Joshua Smith (12)   143
Callum Perry (11)   143
Nicholas Pope (11)   144
Mark Saint (11)   144
Chloe Temple (11)   145
Amy Laidlow (11)   145
Natalie Fitzjohn (11)   146
Bethan Dyer (11)   146
Jessica Warburton (11)   147
Nicholas Garland (11)   147
Catherine Twaite (11)   148
James Smith (11)   148
Victoria Roe (11)   149
Andrew Wand (11)   149
Jade Lane (11)   150
Kerry Battams (11)   150
Daniel Morris (11)   151
Jack Gandy (11)   151
Tom Price (11)   152
Aimee Hunt (11)   152
Karandeep Sahota (11)   153
Dominic Vidler-Green (11)   153

Alice Penney (11)	154
Joshua Edwards (11)	154
Stephanie Gostling (12)	155
George Hughes (11)	155
David Jackson (11)	156
James Mason (12)	156
Elizabeth Manning (11)	156
Lidia Dodsworth (11)	157
Richard Powell (11)	157

Trinity House School, Hull

Mark Goff (11)	158
Jack Barker (11)	158
Harvey Cosway (11)	158
Lewis Burns (11)	159
Alex McCoy (11)	159
Aiden Andrews-McDermott (11)	160
Billy Kinnersley (11)	160
Patrick Sheriff (12)	161
Ryan Lamb (11)	161
Jamie Walters (11)	162
Lewis Brady (11)	162
Daniel Barker (11)	163
Richard Appleton (11)	163
Ross Williamson (11)	164
Ashley Rogers (11)	164
Oliver Collins (11)	165
Joe Gay (11)	165
Michael Pearson (11)	166
Sultan Idmisov (11)	166
Reece Woods (11)	166
Ryan Barr (11)	167

Vale of Ancholme Technology College, Brigg

Thomas Hooton (13)	167
Josh Shaw (12)	168
Aimee-Lauren Westwood (12)	168
James Clark (12)	169
Richard Smelt (12)	169
Jake Beasley (13)	170
Daniel Smith (12)	170

Adelle Grierson (14)   171
Amy Thompson (13)   172
Jade Ronald & Charlotte Robinson (13)   172
Rebecca Cheong (12)   173
Alicia Rhodes (12)   173
Jasmine Richardson & Lauren Russell (11)   174
Tim Metcalfe (12)   174

The Poems

Children In Need

C hildren require support and aid
H appiness can be portrayed
I llness and pain defeated
L ove and care distributed
D reariness and dark expelled
R adiance and light propelled
E njoyment and effervescence made
N o fears are longer laid

I lluminations of life so bright
N ew aspirations reach a higher height

N o one needs to be terrified
E xtra help has arrived
E ternity and destiny at a new fall
D istribution of love dissipated to all.

Ramandeep Kaur (16)

France

F rance is a great country
R ight in the middle of Europe
A beautiful city is Paris
N ever can lose a tourist's attention
C ircle Paris and you will find a lot of amusements, like the
E iffel Tower, which takes your breath away.

Taranom Movahedi (12)

Food

Food is really quite the treat
Fun to make and fun to eat
There's lots of different types of food
To really get you in the mood
If you're sad, chocolate's the dish
If you're not, I suggest fish!

Get busy in the kitchen, there's lots to do
So many foods, all for you
Chocolate mousse for you to make
Or a delicious raspberry cake
From ready made meals, two minutes to cook
To a two-hour meal, Sunday dinner or duck.

When you're tired and not in the mood
There's some places to get fast food
If you don't want to go too far
I bet there's a McDonald's wherever you are
A Pizza Hut or Burger King
Everybody's kind of thing!

If fit and trim you want to stay
Remember the magic five a day
For an even better shape
Eat all the veg on your plate
If a heart you want to feed
Fibre's the thing you really need.

Jake Robinson-Steer (13)
Caistor Yarborough School, Caistor

Colours Of The Rainbow

Red is a cherry all juicy and round,
Orange is the morning sun rising from the ground.

Yellow is a fluffy chick, naughty but cute,
Green is my garden pond, a wriggly, slimy newt.

Blue is the colour of tears when you cry,
Indigo is that of the midnight sky.

Violet is my poor dead mouse,
Who used to run around my house.

Rainbows remind me of happy days,
In many, many happy ways!

Alex Jewitt (13)
Caistor Yarborough School, Caistor

Homeless In Winter

Sculptured outline as perfect as a statue.
Incredible eyes twinkling like stars in the night sky.
Moves gracefully, like a swan moving swiftly by.
Isolated from everything except the chilly wind and snow.
Longing to have a home and be loved like a lost puppy.
Encased in only a pair of tatty jeans and a thick, blue, woolly jumper.
She is lonely,
She is cold,
She is homeless in winter.

Emily Tramaseur (13)
Caistor Yarborough School, Caistor

Metaphors

She is a hot cappuccino
She is a red rose
She is the colour lilac
She is a hot lasagne
She is a lampshade

She is a hot cup of tea
She is a carnation
She is the colour red
She is a sofa

She is like a glass of champagne all bubbly and nice
She is a white lily
She is the colour blue
She is a hot apple pie
She is a cushion

She is a cup of cocoa all hot and tasty
She is a daisy all pretty and white
She is the colour red, all warm inside
She is a spicy curry
She is a bed
She is . . . ?

Sarah Shepherdson (13)
Caistor Yarborough School, Caistor

My Simile Poem

His eyes are like stars in the night sky
His nose is like a big, fat, round pie
His figure is like a lanky tree
His face is like a sweet pea
His ears are pointy and flat
That's why most of the time he's seen wearing a hat
He's like an angel floating through Heaven
He's my angel, it's my Heaven.

Chloe Tatam (13)
Caistor Yarborough School, Caistor

He Is

He is a Mitsubishi Spider
As you're gripping to the seat.
He is 2 Fast 2 Furious
As the tyres skid on the street.

He is the colour red
As the sun sets in the sky.
He is a refreshing drink of water
When your mouth feels dry.

He is hot, crispy bacon
Frying on a grill,
He means all these things to me
And he always will.

Joe Thompson (13)
Caistor Yarborough School, Caistor

Up Above!

Stars shining in the sky,
    Like lights flashing on a Christmas tree.
Clouds floating round the sky,
    Like candyfloss blowing in the wind.
Rain falling from the sky,
    Like tears from an eye.
Lightning flashing in the sky,
    Like a torch in the darkness.

Up above there are wonderful things.

Leona Brown (13)
Caistor Yarborough School, Caistor

My Poem

W inter's coming,
  I ce-cold mornings,
  L ighting fires,
  L ogs burning,
  I ce skating on frozen ponds,
A nimals hibernating,
M ugs of steaming hot chocolate.

S ummer holidays to plan,
H ot days ahead,
A nimals come out to play,
K eeping safe in the sun,
E vening sunsets,
S wimming in the sea,
P icnics in the parks,
E ndless BBQs,
A lways wear suncream,
R unning through the meadows,
E ating lots of ice creams.

Laura Mitchell (11)
Casterton Community College, Great Casterton

Chelsea

Great minds are used every day,
But have to be used in the right way.
I know someone who does it correct,
Chelsea always gives it effect.

She is always there,
Whenever you're feeling bare,
She's Chelsea!

Sarah Webb (11)
Casterton Community College, Great Casterton

Great Minds

Great minds,
Imagination running wild,
Your brain overpowers you
And the way you think.

Great minds,
Are like powerful machines,
Constantly working,
When we can't see it.

Great minds,
Filled with extraordinary powers,
That may have never
Been discovered before.

Joseph Dulieu (11)
Casterton Community College, Great Casterton

Great Mind Like Rooney

There was a lad called Rooney
Who ran and ran like a loony.
He was the age of eighteen,
But no greater skill have we seen.
For he was a footballer ahead of years,
Bringing great hope and plenty of tears.
To England, our fantastic team,
Will Rooney bring our lifelong dream?
To win the World Cup is our goal
And Rooney will play an important role.
He is our country's greatest find,
A footballer with skill and what a mind!

Thomas Birks (11)
Casterton Community College, Great Casterton

The Great Mind

The great mind is a brilliant gift
It's like a million unknown colours just waiting to be mixed
It's like a flickering candle that will never die
Even when there is nothing to burn on
The great mind is like a river flowing with ideas
Just waiting to be caught.

A great mind is something to be proud of
Even if the body doesn't work
It's like a moon always floating around freely into outer space
It's like a net always catching ideas
That float around untouched and unused
The great mind is like a puzzle never to be completed or solved.

The mind is always growing
Even when the body is not
It's like a doorway, always open to new pieces of knowledge
It's like a bird, always letting its imagination fly freely
A great mind is like a cheetah
Always growing and running freely.

Jake Loomes (11)
Casterton Community College, Great Casterton

Big Britain

Johnny Vegas, Peter Kay,
Even 'Little Britain' I must say.
Really as funny as each other,
Sillier than Jake's little brother.

They all have similar jokes,
Johnny even smokes!
Peter's released another DVD,
It's still better than a normal CD.

Fun they always are,
Some as bright as a star.
They never disappoint us,
Comedians are they!

Nick Cunnington (11)
Casterton Community College, Great Casterton

The Super Criminal Mastermind

It's the Super Criminal Mastermind,
Fast, thin and extraordinarily fit,
Even though he is not that good or kind,
He can jump over a 50 foot pit.

In the night he hides in the dark shadows,
Like a huge, hungry black widow waiting,
Until he finally gets up and goes
And steals the precious masterpiece painting.

He keeps his identity under wraps,
He always makes certain he's in disguise,
And never really gets caught,
Perhaps because he is extremely shrewd and wise.

He uses his intelligence to find,
It's the Super Criminal Mastermind!

Daniel Wright (11)
Casterton Community College, Great Casterton

Friends!

My first friend is Sarah,
She's funny, silly and tall,
She's really helpful,
She's really cool.

My second is Kirsty,
She's weird, silly and small,
She's funny,
But she's cool.

My third friend is Harriet,
She's really funny,
She's really sweet,
She's only five and she is really alive.

Chelsea Cantwell (11)
Casterton Community College, Great Casterton

Coma

I lay in the dark old ward,
My body lying lifeless,
My arms and legs so still,
But my mind is always working.

I lay for many hours,
Listening to my mother's sorrow for me,
I felt my heart breaking,
I couldn't take it much longer.

I kept assuring myself that I would come out of it,
That I would see life again,
But the only life that I could see,
Was the life that is in my mind.

I felt the years go by,
The sorrow that lay ahead,
I felt my mind taking control,
Full of thoughts and ideas.

Thoughts kept crawling up my spine,
Will I ever see daylight?
And if I do,
Will I ever remember it?

Someday I'll come out,
Out of this horrible hell,
Knowing about my mind,
And the things it did as well!

Holly Duerden (11)
Casterton Community College, Great Casterton

A Hallowe'en Alphabet

A is for a scream, when you get scared,
B is for *boo!*
C is for the killer candy that you get,
D is for Dracula, with all his bats,
E is for everyone being scary,
F is for freaky frogs,
G is for ghastly ghosts,
H is for hairy beasts, always tangled up,
I is for an inky monster, bulging and blue,
J is for jellyfish, a stinging monster,
K is for killing kats,
L is for lunging bats,
M is for minky monsters,
N is for nearly dead,
O is for 'oh help me',
P is for killer peas (they are vegetables),
Q is for queen of all ghouls,
R is for really scary,
S is for stupidly scary, spooky stories,
T is for the-monsters-under-the-bed,
U is for ugly ghouls,
V is for very scary vampires,
W is for 'why are you screaming?'
X is for extra scary,
Y is for 'you're dead',
Z is for zombie, coming to get you!

Emma Rice (11)
Casterton Community College, Great Casterton

Friends

Friends are cool,
Friends are fab,
Friends are exciting,
Friends are mad.

My friends are funny,
They make me laugh,
We play outside
And work in class.

Friends are helpful,
When trouble comes,
We tell our friends,
But not our mums.

When I have a troubled night,
My friends will listen to my dreams,
They share my problems and my thoughts,
Then explain to me what it all means,
When my friends cry I help them out.

Charlotte Francis (11)
Casterton Community College, Great Casterton

Autumn

Autumn,leaves go swaying down,
They hit the ground and make a sound.
Feeling shivers make you sneeze
And a light, gentle cough like the autumn breeze.
The trees are now bare,
So you must be aware.
The rest of the leaves go swaying down
And get tangled up in your hair,
When autumn comes, beware.

Charmaine Benton (11)
Casterton Community College, Great Casterton

Christiano Ronaldo

C ocky and clever
H andsome and lovely
R ich and famous
I rresistible
S peedy
T alented
I nteresting life
A wesome
N ever gets sent off
O pens people's minds

R ough and tough
O n a lot of adverts
N ever loses the ball
A mazing
L isbon
D elivers good balls
O verall the best.

Emma Ward (12)
Casterton Community College, Great Casterton

Joey Cole

Plays football like a good footie master
Runs down the wing going faster and faster.

Kicks a ball like a bullet from a gun
The keeper was blinded by the big, bold sun.

He scores some as good as Beckham
Now he's gone out there to go get 'em.

Ben Lewis (12)
Casterton Community College, Great Casterton

My Great Mind!

My mind is as calm as the sea sometimes,
And as wild as a bee sometimes.
It's as clever as a chimp sometimes
And that's why I love my mind.

My mind is as funny as my hair sometimes
And as talented as my feet sometimes,
And also as weird as my brother
And that's why I love my mind.

My mind is as creative as my fingers sometimes
And as peaceful as a hymn,
And as caring as my mother sometimes
And that's why I love my mind!

A mind can be anything, as long as you enjoy it
And that's why I love *my* mind!

Jake Walton (12)
Casterton Community College, Great Casterton

Rachel Stevens

R achel is the best
A ctress
C lever
H eroine
E nergetic
L egend!

S Club 7
T alented
E xcellent
V ictorious
E xciting
N ever gives up
S inger!

Kate Billson (12)
Casterton Community College, Great Casterton

A Great Mind - Martin Luther King

M artin Luther King,
A great mind who could sing.
R espected the white people and the black people,
T o stick together as one big family,
I n the United States of America,
N othing in his way.

L oving his family dearly,
U ntil his dying day,
T he people of America did not agree,
H e carried on in every way,
E ven when there was hate,
R eaching his goal, great!

K eeping his promise to his family,
I n being successful he could see,
N othing got in his way ever,
G reat men go on in our hearts forever.

Zoë Sargeant (12)
Casterton Community College, Great Casterton

The Great Mind

Her mind is thinking, thinking, thinking it through,
But what is she thinking in this very room?
The cogs are twirling, turning, turning in her head,
Sitting in the corner, my thoughts are now unravelling like
                                        cotton thread.
I am looking for an expression, looking for a clue,
Now my mind is jammed, like the world's stickiest glue!
I am trying to find an answer, that's what I'm trying to find,
But I just can't help it, she has a great mind.

Amelia Shippey (11)
Casterton Community College, Great Casterton

Great Minds

I am asthmatic, but I can run far,
I can run for miles on grass or tar.
I've had many accidents in my time,
If I carry on, then I will feel fine.

When I am nervous I think alone,
I close my eyes and think of home.
I run my marathons feeling proud,
I don't stop until I impress the crowd.

Keeping up the effort, I try my best,
But sometimes I have to just stop and rest.
My story is like the tortoise and the hare,
But if I am quick, I can get anywhere.

I have achieved my goals many times,
But now I've gone to the back of the line.
But if I think positive then I know I will win,
So come on guys, Paula Radcliffe's in!

Katie Youngs (12)
Casterton Community College, Great Casterton

Djibral Cisse

D ominant
J olly
I nspirational
B rilliant at football
R aring to go
A mazing
L iverpool!

C an't stop scoring goals
I maginative
S mart
S upreme
E nergetic!

Brydon Frith (12)
Casterton Community College, Great Casterton

A Great Mind

One woman in the world inspires me,
She is musical and talented.
The first letter of her name is a C,
She puts inspired thoughts into my head.

She plays a gleaming sax,
She plays so very well,
She reaches the very max
And makes the world feel swell.

The sax she holds is gold,
As golden as the sun above.
When I hear her play so bold,
It makes me feel full of love.

Her name is Candy Dulfer
And because she is so fab
At playing the sax loud and softer,
Learning the sax makes me glad.

Jessica Blaes (12)
Casterton Community College, Great Casterton

Our English Coasts

While the sheep were
        Sleeping,
The farmer said they should be
        Eating.
They lay flat on their
        Backs,
They always stayed in a
        Pack.
They wouldn't do what they were
        Told,
So the farmer gave up and
        Sold them.

Tom Gregg (11)
Casterton Community College, Great Casterton

Great Minds

Somebody terrible, who's horrid or mean,
Could have a great mind, like you or me.
But we would use it to make *good* things happen,
Whereas others might use it to create bad things and sadden
The lives of people old and young,
To make them lose a daughter or son.
Or anyone in fact, anywhere in the world,
From a lowly peasant, to a very grand earl.
So this is the message: be aware, be alert,
Cos you never know when you might get hurt.

On the other hand though,
As you probably know,
Not everyone in this world is bad
Or wants to make other people sad.
There are some people in this world who are good,
Who do their best to ensure people should
Lead a happy and cheerful life,
To help them avoid additional strife.
So this is the message: stay calm, stay safe,
And never forget to have lots of faith.

Jessie Harris (11)
Casterton Community College, Great Casterton

Great Minds

As I look at him from above, I see his mind buzzing,
Full of determination, yet honesty and bravery are overflowing.
Suffering because of his actions and still his intelligence is
never-ending,
A genius in his own way, but using his imagination to a disadvantage.

His positive attitude gets him through the pain he and other people
are enduring,
His creativity and courage allows him to do the things he does,
Yet his kindness and generosity seems never to have existed!

Bryony Smithers (11)
Casterton Community College, Great Casterton

J K Rowling's Characters

There was a young wizard called Harry,
His tricks and magic were the best in the land,
He had a close friend and assistant called Carrie,
She was always there to lend a helping hand.

In the town where he lived was a poor boy called Ron,
He dressed in rags and begged for scraps.
One day Harry looked for the boy, but he was gone,
The only thing to do was look and for this he needed his book
                                            of maps.

Hermione was a girl of special ways,
She had parents with no special powers,
Harry was her pal and they spent many happy days,
Together they battled foes and demons over many, many hours.

The world was good with these children in the place,
They made sure that all the world had a smile on their face.

Carrie Enright (12)
Casterton Community College, Great Casterton

Great Minds

I would really like to have a great mind,
I hope I am also happy and kind.
The people I think are really clever,
We'd be great minds together, forever . . .

Wayne Rooney has a blessed pair of feet,
He is a sports star I want to meet.
My dad is really great, quite clever and bright,
He does DIY all day and all night.

Homer Simpson is funny you will find,
But he really does not have a great mind.
The man who first invented the PC,
Surprise, surprise, is related to me!

Thomas Duffin (11)
Casterton Community College, Great Casterton

The Weird Monster

Sometimes he's hot
Sometimes he's cold
Sometimes his head
Wants to explode.
Sometimes he's black
Sometimes he's white
Sometimes he's wrong
Sometimes he's right.
Sometimes he's rich
Sometimes he's poor
Sometimes a tramp
Comes knocking at his door.
Sometimes he's good
Sometimes he's bad
Then he goes stupid
Then he goes mad.

This is the end,
So don't let the poem drive you round the bend!

Ben McClarnon (11)
Casterton Community College, Great Casterton

Spellings

Why is speling so very, very hard?
Why can't I spel a thing?
If only speling woz mi way,
Then every1 wood bee able too do it!
My way ov speling wood chang revolushun,
All the kids in the world wood bee able too spel,
And all the adults and teachers woodn't,
They shood praise me way of speling,
All around the world!

Emily Rowbotham (11)
Casterton Community College, Great Casterton

My Dad

My dad has a really great mind,
As well as being funny and kind.

On my birthday and at Christmas, my dad totally spoils me,
He's taken me to see Man U, so he had to pay the match fee.

Dad is one of the staff for my football team, so he takes the training,
Even when it's raining.
He takes me to matches on a Sunday morning
And when Mum wakes me at eight thirty, I'm always still yawning.

He takes me on good holidays like to the Maldives and Florida,
And when we get to the airport we go down a corridor.

Whenever I'm stuck with my homework, he always helps me
And it is usually after tea.

My dad has the coolest car of anyone I know,
It is a Jaguar soft-top and it's the opposite to slow.

Sam Swann (12)
Casterton Community College, Great Casterton

Jimi Hendrix

J   imi Hendrix
I   s
M   y
I   dol.

H   e is
E   xcellent on the guitar
N   ever
D   ead in my mind
R   ocked concerts
I   nspiring
e X   cellence.

Jamie Rowlatt (12)
Casterton Community College, Great Casterton

Mona Lisa

The crackles of paint,
The dry, crusty eyes of a human being,
The silky, yet crispy hair.

Mona Lisa's stare.

Her soft, milky face begins to turn grey,
Her pasty face ages with beauty,
Her delicate lips run across her face like a stream of love.

Mona Lisa's stare.

The light that shines upon her begins to darken,
Her dress begins to disappear.

Mona Lisa's stare.

As the picture starts to go,
No one forgets her smile,
That's Mona Lisa's stare!

Sarah-Mae Yardley (11)
Casterton Community College, Great Casterton

Above The Clouds

Looking down on these great minds,
Seeing things not many see,
Many people,
Many talents - lighting up the world
Masses of people sparkling with imagination.
Everyone has something special,
From the sky's point of view,
Everyone's a genius!

Jade Tebbutt (11)
Casterton Community College, Great Casterton

Muhammed Clay

Cassius Clay
Got his own way
In the ring
When the bell went
Ding, ding, ding.

When he got in the ring
He was on fire
He made it look easy
As if he had caught a liar.

Mr Clay went from *hero* to *zero*
With his family of hatred.

Muhammed Ali was his name
He was a star to people
But to family was shamed.

Now he's a poor old man with Parkinson's
But in his time he knocked out some big guns.

Jacob McClarnon (11)
Casterton Community College, Great Casterton

David Beckham

David Beckham, he's the best,
He likes playing football and to impress.
Thinking quick is also his trick.

All he needs are his wife, money and style,
David Beckham is so wild.
He scores the goals for all of his fans.

Sam Dobbs (12)
Casterton Community College, Great Casterton

David Beckham

D estroys other players with his free kicks
A bility to win all the games
V aluable to every team
I mpressive to every team manager
D ominates the goal when he scores

B etter and better as he improves
E xcellent at every pass
C lose to being the best player in the world
K icks the ball like the best
H ated by the other teams
A mazing to watch
M iles better than the rest.

Jordan Holland (12)
Casterton Community College, Great Casterton

Aileen

A bsolutely
I n control. Very
L ikeable.
E xtra organized.
E nergetic.
N icest, the neatest,
   Most calm, confident
   Person you'd ever know.

   She's my sister and
   She has not just a great mind,
   But the *greatest mind!*

Heather McClelland (11)
Casterton Community College, Great Casterton

My Cat

Her sleek, white paws crept across the ground,
She looked left and right and this is what she found.

A bird in a tree, some mice as well,
She jumped on the fence and nearly fell.

She went for the bird at a slick pace,
When the bird turned round, you should have seen its face.

It flew away fast because of the sight,
My cat chased it with all her might.

She gave up quickly after,
She chased the mice, which were dafter.

The point of this poem is that,
I have a fierce, daft cat.

Gemma Sinfield (11)
Casterton Community College, Great Casterton

Dec

Whenever Dec is on TV, he is the most
Funniest,
Brightest,
Most intelligent,
A great sense of humour,
Skilled,
Has a large memory,
Very confident and last of all,
Always comes up with the most creative ideas.

Rosanna Williams (11)
Casterton Community College, Great Casterton

David Beckham

D avid is:
A nice
V ictorious
I ntelligent
D etermined

B rilliant
E nthusiastic
C hallenging
K ind
H appy
A mazing
M an.

Luke Fox (12)
Casterton Community College, Great Casterton

Great Minds

G ood for solving mysteries . . . Sherlock Holmes
R eading instead of watching TV . . . school children
E xcellent when being creative . . . my art teacher
A lways keeps on going . . . Paula Radcliffe
T alkative, a good sense of humour . . . me!

M ind of a bullet . . . Albert Einstein
I n the news . . . Tony Blair
N aturally kind . . . Pudsey bear
D etermined in his game . . . David Beckham
S umming it up: a great mind comes in all shapes and sizes.

Amber Buckley (11)
Casterton Community College, Great Casterton

Dogs Are The Best

Dogs are sweet
And cuddly,
Dogs are the best.

Dogs are Man's best friend,
They are kind,
Dogs are the best.

People like dogs,
Dogs like people,
Dogs are the best.

Dogs love to play
In the dirt,
Dogs are the best!

Louise Mossom (11)
Casterton Community College, Great Casterton

The Great Mind Of Thierry Henry

Thierry Henry is my hero.
The other team will have the score of zero.

He's so aware of where the goal is,
The defender will not know where the ball is.

He is such a teammate
And he's never overweight.

His brain is truly amazing,
He doesn't even need to do any training.

Sam Bacon (11)
Casterton Community College, Great Casterton

I Can't Do It

'Miss, I can't do it.
Miss, what do you do?
Miss, how do you do it?'
'Did you not listen?
I'm not telling you!'

'Miss, I can't do it.
Miss, what is the title?
What does this say?
I did listen.'
'I'm still not telling you!'

'Miss, I can't do it.
Miss, what is this?
Miss, this is impossible.
I can't do this.'

'It's not impossible.
It's only maths.
You do it like this
And that is that.'

Thomas Kellett (11)
Casterton Community College, Great Casterton

Sunset

Red, yellow, orange
Are all mixed together
Slowly rising, in the sky.

When it sets
The colours look lovely
Then evening comes
And the sun goes down.

The sky gets darker
The sun disappears
The night has begun
And the sun has gone.

Rosie Barker (12)
Casterton Community College, Great Casterton

The Battle Of Hastings

In the deafening silence,
The icy cold, piercing winds
Lash against the soldiers' bodies.

The horrid conditions
Of the cramped, frightened men,
Fills them with worry and anger.

The desolate space,
Bridging the two sides,
Is suddenly filled with noise.

Rage overtakes them,
They charge, armed with danger,
The fears open into their eyes.

Older men fearless,
But young men laugh at danger
And they are cut down like weeds.

Hours later,
Row upon row,
Bodies wait to be accepted.

Adam Purcell (11)
Casterton Community College, Great Casterton

Ant And Dec

A nt and Dec
N othing but silly
T wo funny men, that drive you round the bend

&

D iscovering their talent
E very Saturday morning on TV
C hunks and chunks of laughter from me.

Megan Hooper (11)
Casterton Community College, Great Casterton

Fire-Breathing Beasts

D anger lurking in the air,
R oaring sounds run through my hair,
A s the tension begins to rise,
G igantic sights soon strike my eye.
O pening my eyes some more, I see a *beast,*
N o one wants to be his feast.
S oaring through the air so cold,
   The dragon flies as he is bold.

Debra Czornookyj (11)
Casterton Community College, Great Casterton

Dizzy

I stood outside watching the fireworks,
How they lit up the midnight sky.
The sparklers sparkled like fairies,
The Catherine wheels made a scary noise.
I stood there looking at them,
They made me dizzy.

Chloe Berry (11)
Casterton Community College, Great Casterton

Bats

Bats are black,
Bats are brown,
Bats swoop and dodge around.
Bats live in caves,
Bats eat fruit,
They are both different,
But bat's that!

Jacqui Pretlove (11)
Casterton Community College, Great Casterton

Fall Of Struggles

On foot through fields of lostness,
Face up and eyes to the sun,
Searching through what can't be seen,
For a limit that hasn't begun.

Wicked impediments clawing at any integrity,
Dampening lamps clutch the days,
Arduous steps head yet further from the beginning,
Faintness and ill hope precede the ways.

Thoughts that haunt even the last breath,
To conquer what's left in the lands,
What was desired through those dying eyes,
For the ever empty dust-covered hands.

This is where we stand.
All this is where we stand.

Ashraf Ebrahim (17)
Dixons City Technology College, Bradford

Contemplating Suicide

I see myself falling. Off
Eyes wonder transcending -
I hear my sins singing selfishly cursing!
Clouds clouding, as they do . . .
My body's stitches ripping from the seamless spirit
As my mind is swelling inside my head!
An intangible somebody claws my thoughts
Whirling dervishes internally twirling,
Knocked! Against a labyrinth wall -
Unable to find an escapism. Trembling
With insanity, as the sky continues to sky on . . .
I'm flying so delicately on this
Ungravitational sphere.
A cowering feather like a ghostly breath
In a spiralling tendril of white smoke . . .

Kamal Hussain (18)
Dixons City Technology College, Bradford

Not Waving, But Drowning

(Inspired by 'Not Waving, But Drowning' by Stevie Smith)

In the blue and bonny sea,
You see the children out to play.
I think I'll go and join them now,
Play out in the ocean wide.

I'll wave to you,
I'll call to you,
I'll wave to you,
I'll call to you.

I've had a good time,
But now I want to come back.
The tide is pulling me out,
I don't know what to do.

You are waving,
You are calling,
You are waving,
You are calling.

In your eyes I'm waving,
Waving for you.
But in my eyes I'm drowning,
Not waving, but drowning,
Drowning, drowning, drowning not waving.

I've called to you,
I've waved to you.
You've called for me,
You've waved at me.

I'm in too deep,
I've got nowhere to go.
Please help me now,
I'm calling for you.
Calling out for the last time.
Help me!

Emma Parfitt (13)
Dixons City Technology College, Bradford

Agony Speaks

I grow tired,
Trying to fathom your mind,
So intrinsically grey,
Trying to heed your strangled thoughts,
Beckon your untrained ear.

I grow desperate,
Exposed, to the sun bleeding light,
To the valley that cleaves,
To the wind that lashes,
And the rain that slides, devoid of mercy,
Into my eyes, my dull orbs.

I grow weary,
Contorted with pain,
Pecked by the crows.
I die, am reborn,
Only to expire once more,
Before your indifference.

I grow quiet,
Unable to be wrenched,
From the bitter pursuit of nothing,
From the bitter pull of wanting too great a thing.
Hanging like vapour,
All for your cause.

Please. Burst your narrow banks,
Speak my name, let it course down your face,
The intonation sparkling in the flush of my smile.
Say to me: *You have half my heart, please return it,*
And here, you take half of mine.

Katie Sutcliffe (17)
Dixons City Technology College, Bradford

Shroud Of Shadows

Enter the alley, freeze for a bit,
A foul-smelling gutter, water makes a drip,
And a slight breeze brushes past your face,
The hulking wheelie bin, garbage at its base.

Now, the rain comes down, a flash of light,
A rumble of thunder, and lightning so bright.
The wetness beats down; you've got nowhere to hide,
The world now looks like it is turning to the dark side.

Now you hear whimpering, of something scared,
You rush to the scene with the sound you heard,
A tiny tabby, so small and sweet,
Then its face turns to someone you never want to meet.

Then, you hear chatting in the darkest black,
Your mind whispers to you, saying, 'Don't! Go back!
Go back and don't turn back! Please walk away!
Come back again when it is a brighter day!'

But you ignore the cries, coursing through your mind,
You enter the dark, open mouth, leaving life behind,
Now, shadows appear, chuckling and chatting,
Coming and going, swinging and swaying.

You clutch your heart, it's beating fast,
You take another step, and then at last,
The figures turn to you, your confidence is low,
You're caught in the wrath of the *Shroud of Shadows!*

Richard Bartlett (11)
Dixons City Technology College, Bradford

Waiting

Sitting in the trenches
Waiting, waiting
Sitting in the train station
Waiting, waiting
Been given the order
Waiting, waiting
Sitting in the living room
Waiting, waiting
Running through no-man's land
Waiting, waiting
Making munitions
Waiting, waiting
Seeing comrades falling
Waiting, waiting
Listening to the radio for news of her loved one
Waiting, waiting
Caught in the barbed wire
Waiting, waiting
Sitting in silence
Waiting, waiting
Bang!
Waiting, waiting
Receiving the letter
No more waiting.

Jonathan Rainer (12)
Dixons City Technology College, Bradford

Dreams

On and on the river bends,
Flowing towards the sea.
Its spirit free in motion,
'Twas my heart that captured thee.

A seldom sense of happiness,
Like a mountain and the spring,
Becomes the eternal drink for us,
The water of the king.

Magic fountains, pools and rain,
Like a giant shower in a tree,
Collects up all the fountains' rain,
And all the power of me.

So dream and dream until that day,
When all your dreams come true,
But remember all your struggles,
As you're searching for the truth.

And if you see that river,
Flowing towards the sea,
Don't shed a tear, for happiness,
Was the soul that captured me.

Aaron Newland (14)
Dixons City Technology College, Bradford

Winter, The Predator

Through the neglected glades,
Frisks Winter, the predator,
All colour fades
As it gallops through the forest.

Far through the distance,
Its Siberian talons crash and thunder,
Until many primitive branches,
Are torn asunder.

The rain reynards creeps,
To its hole near the river,
The bare leaves fall
And the crude trees shiver.

As Night trotted from the ground,
It hides each tree from its brother
And each dying sound reveals yet another.
It's Winter, the predator,
Which capers through the neglected glades,
Snarling with its polar jaws,
While all colour fades.

Mohammed Anis (11)
Dixons City Technology College, Bradford

Born Again

Haunted yet alive
These spirits crowd my mind
Surround me with poignant icicles
Unleashing their rapture
To rebuke breathlessly.
Beginning with what can be sensed
They dismember me
Limb by limb
Thought by thought
Until I know nothing of my present
But am relentlessly flung
To live in their past.

Sumera Kauser (17)
Dixons City Technology College, Bradford

The Bully

It was my fault,
Really it was,
Nothing can change that,
I couldn't even run.

I stood there watching,
Watching her cry,
If I'd been honest,
She'd still be alive.

Vaishali Mistry (12)
Dixons City Technology College, Bradford

Lardentine

Not something chewy,
Not something hard,
All I give you is a block of lard.
Why? You ask.
The answer's easy.
Cos it makes you nice 'n' greasy.

You always liked to eat cowpat,
But doesn't it taste better with a big blob of fat?
When I leave you,
Your heart is aching,
So use the lard to cook your bacon.

You tell me I'm your ideal man,
Please put the lard in the frying pan.
I will always love you,
I will always be true,
The packet is coloured red, white and blue.

The only thing it gives,
Is a heart attack,
But it's only 47p a pack.
When you're with me your heart is red,
But the lard will make you stiff and dead.

You are dead now, cold and hard,
So I'll finish off your half-eaten lard.

Antony Lifsey (17)
John Leggott College, Scunthorpe

Rejection

My life crumbles at my feet
As the world turns against me
And like dark clouds approaching from the horizon
The end has now begun.

Eerie shadows stretch across the plains
Like the grip of darkness across a soul
The muscle of the heart although it is strong
Is still as fragile as life itself.

Now my heart lies upon the floor
Still marked with the tread of a trusted soul
Withered and cold it lies there now
With only the grip of rejection to keep it warm.

The bitter pain bestowed on me
From one as sweet as anyone can be
Will now forever linger on
Until the end has come and gone.

Devon Warner (17)
John Leggott College, Scunthorpe

Simple Words Of Warning

Talking thus may be a sin
Yet imagination is from within
Fruitful seeds is how it tends to grow
But manic thoughts is what you now sow
I do not write to mock or scorn
A note to you just to warn
That thoughts and deeds are separate things
And good words fly on angels' wings
Past memories here are devils done
We'll fight the battle, it shall be won
For now at least you're on your own
But yet I know you are never alone
A mother's love I now do send
Your torment which I hope will end
And if again your demons rise
May truth be told with lies, with lies.

Gina Davies (17)
John Leggott College, Scunthorpe

IVF Baby

Hello world
You can see when I open my eyes
I'm a miracle
Those two people deserve me
More than anyone else
And as I scream I'm already four years old
A twin of the brother I'll never know.

Hello Mum
I know when I look in your eyes
All the pain we've caused
All twelve of us
Lying in the Arctic for a chance at life
Is that why we're crying together?
Our meeting - four years delayed.

Hello teacher
I hope you got the note
I reckon by the red round your eyes you did
My mum explained who I was
And how I became
And I hope you'll understand
Why nobody can play rough with me.

Hello brother
I heard about your story
I filled in the gaps for you
Nothing's ever fair
We can't choose how we become
I looked in the mirror and thought:
Product of science
Life suspended
　　　　When I should have been living.

Danielle Sempers (18)
John Leggott College, Scunthorpe

Flames Of War

Run along children
Play your games of war
Shoot your guns
Made of sticks
'N' hope you escape
The flames of war

Play together little boys
Play your games
Where guns are toys
'N' pray you escape
The flames of war

Hunt with your father, eldest son
Shoot at animals
They can't shoot back
For hope has failed you
And you cannot escape
The flames of war

Now fight and die, men of war
Slaughter your equals
'N' shed not a single tear
For you live within
The flames of war

You brought us victory
It may seem
Yet on the ground
Your tombstone sits
Broken and shattered
To remind us all
No one can escape
The flames of war.

Sarah Stevenson (16)
John Leggott College, Scunthorpe

Within A Dream

Every
Movement she made,
Every breath she slowly sighed
Touched the skin of blushed cheeks.
Her tulip
Hands explore his terrain.
The intimate
Sensation of
A kiss, a scent, a stroke;
Burst open the heart
Felt lust within.
A state of abstraction
Bearing a misleading
Trance of counterfeit senses,
Deceiving as one
His mind, his soul, his body, his taste,
His eyes dilate
And explode.

Breathing in deep,
The chillness of blue oxygen
Punching against the lining of his lungs
Captures the essence of cold air
And wakes his sleeping body.

Jacky Wong (18)
John Leggott College, Scunthorpe

Asylum

I wander around these blank, white walls
They may think I am wrong in the head
But I keep my sanity encased
I could well end up dead

My sister, she was an addict
Injecting herself with strange fluids
She went mad and fell off a cliff
Saying she was chased by Druids

I hate myself for my misfortune
My soul I have to sell
Because I had to denounce my faith
I may as well go to Hell

I tried to say I was sane
And even confessed my sins
But even though they listened
They still kicked me in the shins

The thing that keeps me calm
Among the violence of those seven
Is that the more one suffers
The closer one gets to Heaven.

Scott Fowler (16)
John Leggott College, Scunthorpe

Remember Me?

Remember me?
You stole my pride away
from under my nose.
Remember how
you looked down on me?
'Not worth the effort,'
you said.

Remember when
you saw me stepping up behind
your shoulder?
Status gained.
Remember who
took your pride away in
your small kingdom?
Mine it became.

Remember why
I gained?
You lost in the
place we came to love.
Remember because
of me I let you
stick around, take my former
throne below.

Remember now?
How I gained, you lost.
Remember the day
doubt crossed your mind?
I came from behind.
Stole victory.

Remember me
saying, 'I won?'
You felt so small,
now you know
the humiliation
of it all.

Remember how, when, why.
Remember me.
Never forget.

James Newcome (16)
Monks' Dyke Technology College, Louth

Fatally Forgotten

Teddy lies threadbare, discarded,
With twisted limbs and contorted, cotton expression.
Is his grimace for his gashed head,
Bleeding wiry stuffing,
Or for his one smashed eye?
Or for being forced to lie in the mass cardboard grave
In the dark attic corner,
Where Doll forever stares and is rendered dumb,
Her cord around her throat?
Memories are gone of when he lay on the comfortable eider,
His bed now is Clown, another victim.
Teddy lies threadbare, discarded, destroyed.

Catherine Watts (16)
Queen Elizabeth's Grammar School, Horncastle

Bonfire Night!

Hear them bang!
See a big crowd in a gang!
Hear children scream,
See fireworks pink and green,
See a clump of colourful stars,
Like Saturn, Jupiter and Mars,
See them sparkle, hear them crackle!

The noise is amazing,
My mum stands gazing,
They look wonderful,
'Cause the sky is dull.

Hear them bang!
See a big crowd in a gang!
Hear babies screaming,
See the sky beautifully gleaming,
Guy Fawkes is getting burnt,
I think this trip was well earnt,
The fire is really big,
He stands as big as big can be,
Looking at him scares me!

Lorna Turner (12)
Queen Elizabeth's High School, Gainsborough

The Clock

A sim-ple clock just ticks and tocks,
The larg-est hand goes round and round,
A clock can hyp-no-tise it can,
A clock looks like a fry-ing pan.

A clock can be in any room,
It ticks and tocks, but does not move,
It stays on the wall for all to see,
And it tells the time just for me.

Dominic Powell (12)
Queen Elizabeth's High School, Gainsborough

Wild Fire

Ssscruchh
The match is alight
And thrown on the heap,
The bonfire burns with all its might.
With a *crack* and a *crick,*
A *boom* and a *bang,*
You calmly feel the flames gently
On your hypnotised, numb face.
Stand and stare, watch and glare
At the flames dancing with such grace
And taking extreme care.
Dying, fading, about to end,
As slowly the wild fire had been tamed
And is going to sleep,
Until next year, when he can play again.

Darcy Martin (12)
Queen Elizabeth's High School, Gainsborough

A Bonfire Night

Look at them whizz,
Look at them fizz,
Orange, blue, pink and green,
Oh, it's such a beautiful scene.
All the colours merge together,
It will stay in my head forever,
All the stars shine out bright,
It is such a memorable night.
The fireworks go bang,
You can hear them clang,
Sizzle, frizzle, crackle, bang,
Me and my friends are watching in a gang.
My friends stand in amazement,
They want to go and give them a compliment,
Oh, it's such a beautiful scene,
Orange, blue, pink and green.

Hannah Balfour (11)
Queen Elizabeth's High School, Gainsborough

Bonfire Night

The bonfire is lit,
Our ears split,
From the sound
Of the fire as we walk round.

The fireworks fly,
Up high in the sky,
The fire's staying still,
Watching from high on a hill.

The colours are bright,
They shine in the night,
They make children go *wow!*
And make the adults ask how?

The fireworks fly,
Up high in the sky,
The fire's staying still,
Falling asleep high on a hill.

The fire is dying,
It's burning down,
Slowly, slowly, children leave,
Waiting for next year to come.

Chloe Smith (11)
Queen Elizabeth's High School, Gainsborough

The Strain Of The Wind

The wind is curling
Around the corners it goes
Whirling and swirling
He's mad and it shows.

He does what he may
Whether wrong or right
'Get out of my way,'
He shouts through the night.

And when it comes today
The wind slows right down
He runs far away
He's now peaceful and sound.

But then he gets snoring
He has started up now
He thought it was boring
So he blasts through the town.

Another day passed away
The wind is ready to go
The wind has gone to play
If he comes again I'll let you know.

Holly Southward (11)
Queen Elizabeth's High School, Gainsborough

The Splash Machine

The sea splashing against the sandy shore
Fish get washed up more and more
The seagulls crow in the early morning
The sea glitters when the sun is dawning.

Colourful jellyfish squiggle and squirm
Seaweed shaped like dead worms
Ocean spray like a garden hose
The brightness of the sun burns your nose.

The smell is fusty, fishy, a delight
The colours of the beach hut are so bright
The sky's cloudless, like a blue piece of paper
I think I might have an ice cream later.

Finally, when the sea gets darker
The sky's been coloured in with a marker
The sun met the sea in the morning
When it was only just dawning.

Kalita Offer (12)
Queen Elizabeth's High School, Gainsborough

Vicious Sea

Slowly he eats at the land,
Pulling chunks out with hungry hands,
Washing over all the sand,
Making destruction wherever he can.

Hitting rocks, spray away,
Seagulls flock day after day.

Pulling pebbles out to sea,
Worn away the lighthouse bay,
Many wish to have their say,
Against the crashing of dismay.

Crawling closer, ever nearer,
Falling closer, getting clearer.

Holly Constable (11)
Queen Elizabeth's High School, Gainsborough

The Pouring Rain

The pitter-patter,
The splitter-splatter
Of the pouring rain,
Oh, what a shame.
Everyone soaking wet,
A cat, a dog and some other pet.
Giant puddles on the ground,
The horrible, horrible, repeated sound.
Splish, splash,
Wish, wash.

Slowly, out of the dark grey clouds,
The sun comes out,
Everyone shouts.
It's finally sunny
And everybody finds it funny.

Jordan Tennant (11)
Queen Elizabeth's High School, Gainsborough

A Windy Day

Out of control winds roaring,
Sleeping men are snoring,
Numb fingers are freezing,
The wind is wheezing.

Winds are smiling smugly,
Bare trees looking ugly,
Hot fires are crackling,
The cruel winds are cackling.

Snowdrifts falling,
Cars start stalling,
The wind will go strong,
All day long.

Mark Picken (11)
Queen Elizabeth's High School, Gainsborough

Nature's Force

A long rumble of thunder.
Crash!
Lightning strikes
And the wind howls its curses to all who will listen,
All who are out on this dark, evil night.

Then thunder claps
And the earth all around shakes violently.
Smouldering black holes cover the ground,
Once clean and healthy.

Towering waves streak across the open sea,
Waves fuming with anger,
Destroying all in their path and trying to wreak
As much havoc as possible before they run out of energy
And collapse back into the sea.

Crash! Crash! Crash!
Lightning strikes an ancient oak.
It *burns* like a great bonfire,
Until it begins to fall.
It *slams* into the ground, never to see another day.

The storm starts to die down,
But the damage has been done.
An area once beautiful has turned into a vast wasteland,
Never to be the same again.

Luke Martin (12)
Queen Elizabeth's High School, Gainsborough

The Firework

Light the lighter,
It gets brighter and brighter,
The Catherine wheel starts to spin and squeal -
But all so slowly it starts to get faster,
While the fence stands solid it supports the master.

Colour changing in twos,
Reds and blues,
Crimson and green,
Great to be seen.

Ear-splitting,
Brain hitting,
Round and round,
Piercing sound,
Colourful crown,
Won't slow down,
Makes you stare,
Hypnotizing glare.

Slowly slowing,
Dims the glowing,
The noise stops,
The spinning stops,
Everything stops as the firework
Burns away.

Danielle Wood (11)
Queen Elizabeth's High School, Gainsborough

Bonfire Night

This is the Bonfire Night,
When the stars shine bright.
Crackle, spit, roar and spark,
Goes the bonfire into the dark.
This is the night that we celebrate,
Because of Guy Fawkes' big mistake.

Like a zoo, the children howl,
To hear a sparkler's magic sounds.
The sky is a big, black sheet,
Guarding us from the sun's scarring heat.
Sparkle, spin, spiral and spark,
The sparklers are making their beautiful mark.

Now the bit we've all been waiting for,
The fireworks' beautiful parade.
There are adults laughing and children clapping,
As the man walks up to the stage.

Bang! And the fireworks are free,
All of the beautiful colours before me,
Are turning into a memory,
That will last forever and a day!

Savannah Bowles (11)
Queen Elizabeth's High School, Gainsborough

Bonfire Night

Bonfire Night,
A delightful sight.
A brilliant place to be
And all the children giggle with glee.
The fireworks are sent,
The last bang ringing in their ears.
Children start to peer,
Wishing to catch one last sight
Of the bonfire's greatest delight.

Lewis Hancock (12)
Queen Elizabeth's High School, Gainsborough

Deep Water

A raging, roaring, vicious storm,
It's coming in an angry form,
Overlapping the feeble waves,
For help is what the beaches crave.
Crushing everything in sight,
Showing overpowering might.

The deep waves are slowly calming,
Swish . . . swosh, settling,
Slowing down, now smooth and steady,
Wish . . . wash, steadying.

Small children coming out to play,
The storm will hit another day,
For today it did not succeed,
Its angry body now shall bleed.

Danielle Smith (11)
Queen Elizabeth's High School, Gainsborough

The Sea

A rolling, rushing, running sea,
A crawling, caving, crushing sea,
Rolling in day after day,
No one on land gets their say.
A crushing sea, taking lives,
People never dare to dive,
In an angry sea.

A soothing, smoothing, sightless sea,
A gentle, glassy, gorgeous sea,
Gently now it comes rolling in,
The rivers and streams are its kin.
Soothing any frayed nerves,
Everyone on Earth knows the purpose it serves,
A life-saving sea.

Emma Goodson (11)
Queen Elizabeth's High School, Gainsborough

Bonfire Night

The bonfire started with an exciting bang,
We're waiting for the firework gang.
One,
Yellow like runny honey,
Two,
Red like sticky jam tarts,
Bang!
Three,
Blue oceans meet,
Four,
Purple and pink blossomed trees,
Five,
Crash!
Catherine wheels go round and round,
Sparklers have no sound . . .
Crash!
Six,
Multicolours like a rainbow,
Seven,
Orange like an amber gemstone,
Eight,
Green like fresh grass,
Nine,
Gold like the winning medal,
Bang!
Calming down now, nearly done,
Leaving the bonfire all alone.

Madison Devine (11)
Queen Elizabeth's High School, Gainsborough

The War

As the army walks up the hill
The archers load their bows to kill
They pull back with mighty strength
To make the arrow fly with length
Up it goes into the sky
Look at it fly
They make men die

The arrows kill many soldiers
Coming down like a storm of boulders
All the archers load again
To make the enemy feel more pain
Up it goes into the sky
Look at it fly
They make men die

The entire enemy ran in retreat
Looks like the archers had given defeat
Many made it back to their home
But the king hadn't made it back to his throne
Up it goes into the sky
Look at it fly
They make men die.

Tom Fenwick (11)
Queen Elizabeth's High School, Gainsborough

The Ocean's Tide

It was a bright winter's day
The ocean was fierce, flinging its spray
No one could catch the running tide
Roaring in and out like a lion with pride.

The only thing to see is sky
With the waves splashing so high
Frothing foam in my face
Rushing through at some pace.

The moonlight appears, wavy, silky and fair
Calming the seas, glistening sweetly everywhere
A sweep of wind dies away
And ripples are silent at the end of the day.

Gemma Burns (11)
Queen Elizabeth's High School, Gainsborough

Bonfire Night

Bonfire Night
The fireworks take flight
What a sight!
The fireworks gather height
Pink, violet and white
The fireworks shoot up
Like a ball from a cannon

We wait for the next
As they connect
To start another show
So the crowd won't go
Spirals, rockets and wonderful wheels
Listen to the children squeal.

Ross Burnett (11)
Queen Elizabeth's High School, Gainsborough

Manwind

The growing wind whispers past -
An almost silent breath, the last.
He picks up through brass keyholes,
Bending round lamp posts.

He is like an angry giant,
Reaching up to snatch roof tiles,
Woken by his terrible roars,
People watch him kick leaves into piles.

Late into the dark night,
Coming soon to morning.
He stops all his howling
And collapses without warning.

For now his terror has ceased,
The wind shows his trailing path,
No more remembered, though he'll be back
To continue his work, his destructive wrath.

Rebecca Gray (11)
Queen Elizabeth's High School, Gainsborough

Bonfire Night

He is an evil man
Who will kill you if he can
Angry as can be
Will have you for his tea

His flashing eyes go up in the sky
Get in the way and you will die
He stamps away, with flames and bangs
His flames are just like fangs.

Matthew Lawson (11)
Queen Elizabeth's High School, Gainsborough

Bonfire Night

Fireworks went up into the sky
Flying long and exploding high
As they went up children smiled
Sparks came down into a glowing pile
Families stood side by side
As if queuing for a roller coaster ride.

The fireworks exploded into amazing colours
It was almost as if it was the sun in summer
Babies were scared as the fireworks went high
They looked as if they were going to die
The loudest firework was the rocket
Although it was so small, it could fit in your pocket.

Now that Bonfire Night is finally finished
All of the fireworks have mysteriously vanished
The noises I heard were very loud
They were almost louder than a football crowd
When Bonfire Night comes round next year
I'm going to make sure I cover my ears!

Andrew McPheat (11)
Queen Elizabeth's High School, Gainsborough

Fantasy Creatures

A werewolf is big and hairy,
On a night with a full moon he can be scary.
A vampire will never die,
He will drink you dry.

Frankenstein is not very bright,
But he puts up a very good fight.
Ghosts are pale white,
They give you a very big fright.

Zombies are dumb,
They can't tell the difference between rubber and gum.
Cyclops have only one eye,
But they enjoy meat pies.

Daniel O'Shea (13)
St Bede's Catholic Grammar School, Bradford

A Lonely Portrait

Here I am all on my own
By myself all alone
People stop, stand and stare
I'm a hollow man, there's no one there

I wish I wasn't so hated and lonely
But the face I put on is so fake and phony
I hang my head down on my chest
Hoping things will turn out for the best

There I hang so pale and worn
My skin is broken, tattered and torn
No one cares if I die
At least I'll be cared for in the sky

Here I am staring at others
Mothers, fathers, sisters and brothers
No one remembers me now
I'm just the man who didn't know how.

Joseph Buchaldzin (13)
St Bede's Catholic Grammar School, Bradford

The Cupboard

I heard a noise coming from the cupboard,
I went to get my fearless brother.
He opened the cupboard,
. . . he died.
I went to get my brave dad,
He opened the bloodstained door,
. . . he died.
I went to get my mum,
She opened the bloodied door,
I heard a screech,
. . . she died.
I stepped over the pond of blood,
I opened the door,
. . . I died.

Ashley McNulty (12)
St Bede's Catholic Grammar School, Bradford

I Hate!

I hate it when there is no sun,
I hate missing out on all the fun.
I hate looking really smart,
I hate people who are good at art.
I hate . . . I hate . . . I hate.

I hate people who play cricket,
I hate people who say 'in it'.
I hate looking at the light,
I hate to be in a fight.
I hate . . . I hate . . . I hate.

I hate it when England lose,
I hate it when I have to choose.
I hate it when I have bad dreams,
I hate eating melty ice creams.
I hate . . . I hate . . . I hate.

I hate it when I pick my nose,
I hate when people wiggle their toes.
I hate it when I have to work,
I hate the people who drive a Merc.
I hate . . . I hate . . . I hate.

But do you want to know the thing I hate most?
I hate things I hate.

Nathan O'Shea (12)
St Bede's Catholic Grammar School, Bradford

Tick Tock Clock

Tick tock clock
The children look out at the clock, tick tock
The bell rings, the children sing
The teachers are relieved
All thanks to the tick tock clock.

Faizhan Hussain (12)
St Bede's Catholic Grammar School, Bradford

Year 8

It's a new start
And a new year,
At least now there
Is nothing to fear.
I know all of the rules
And the size of the stools,
I know the score
And a lot, lot more.

This year I seem to be more brainy,
Because now I've been taught by Mr Delaney.
I'm making a lot of progress,
Instead of being in a bit of a mess.

I've moved from set three,
Into set one,
But there is still some more work
To be done.

Colum Sheridan-Small (12)
St Bede's Catholic Grammar School, Bradford

A Marching Army

We don't march on our knees
Prefer to use our feet
Quicker over mountains
Through the blazing, flaming heat

We tremble in our boots
Marching to our war
Running through the battlefield
They stood still in awe

Firing their guns through the mist
They couldn't see at all
Wishing they were somewhere else
Like dancing at a ball.

Jack Tidswell (12)
St Bede's Catholic Grammar School, Bradford

Tomorrow

When tomorrow starts without me
And I'm not here to see
If the sun should rise and find your eyes
All filled with tears for me

I wish so much you wouldn't cry
The way you did today
While thinking of the many things
We didn't get to say

I know how much you love me
As much as I love you
And each time that you think of me
I know you'll miss me too

But when tomorrow starts without me
Please try to understand
That an angel came and called my name
And took me by the hand

And said my place was ready in Heaven far above
And that I'd have to leave behind
All those I dearly love
But when I walked through Heaven's gates

I felt so much at home
When God looked down and smiled at me
From his great, golden throne
He said, 'This is eternity and all I've promised you.'

Today my life on Earth is past
But here it starts anew
I promise no tomorrow
For today will always last

And since each day's the same way
There's no longing for the past
So when tomorrow starts without me
Don't think we're apart

For every time you think of me
I'm right here in your heart.

Usman Sarwar (12)
St Bede's Catholic Grammar School, Bradford

Pies

What is a pie? So full of meat,
I waste no time its crust to eat.
The gravy squirts on the teacher's blouse,
As I scoff chunks of sheep or cows.
No time for beans, they give me gas,
I just want pies you silly ass.
No time for cakes,
Though they're alright,
I could eat pies,
All through the night.

No time to sing,
No time to dance,
I spy a pie - it's got no chance!
No time to waste, when my mouth can
Close round a pie - I'm such a fan!
I eat them round, I eat them square,
Aw, they're all gone - that's just not fair!

Christopher Riley (12)
St Bede's Catholic Grammar School, Bradford

My Day At School

One morning I went to school,
Thinking it was going to be nothing like cool.
I went to my class to sit in my chair,
But someone behind me touched my hair.
I turned around, was it my friend Dan?
But guess who it was? It was Jackie Chan!

At break he taught me his punch and his kick,
Because a guy hated me called Mick.
At the end of the day Jackie had to go home,
But Mick didn't and nicked my phone.
I did what Jackie did - the kick and the punch,
Now he doesn't pick on me because I made him throw up his lunch.

Mark Furniss (12)
St Bede's Catholic Grammar School, Bradford

Cars!

There are so many to choose from,
Which one should you choose?
There are fast Ferraris,
Super Subarus,
Magnificent Mazdas,
Beautiful Bentleys,
Mad Masseratis,
Jingly Jaguars,
Vicious Vipers,
Creepy Cobras,
Brilliant BMWs,
Marvellous Mercedes,
Furious Fiats,
Ace Aston Martins and many more.
So remember,
The next time you go to buy a car,
Don't just buy one,
Buy them all!

Luke Whitehead (12)
St Bede's Catholic Grammar School, Bradford

Daffodils

And as I wandered by the lake
I saw those golden, dancing heads
I wish the moment would not break
   Too free to lie in flower beds.

This fast pace life which we lead
We sometimes miss the simple things
We may be blinded by our greed
And do not see what nature brings
Just look at clouds and suns and hills
And simple things like daffodils.

Toby Romano (12)
St Bede's Catholic Grammar School, Bradford

The Sun

The sun is big,
The sun is bright,
The sun is warm,
The sun is light!

The sun lightens up the world,
So everyone can see,
It tans our skin nice and brown,
Both you and me!

The sun can also be a pain,
When it burns our skin,
People hide in the shade,
But they don't always win!

The sun makes us feel so good,
I wish it was here every day,
But winter comes, it goes away,
But never mind, it will soon be back to stay!

Jordan Watt (12)
St Bede's Catholic Grammar School, Bradford

I Wonder

What will I be when I grow old?
An artist, architect, I've been told.
I wonder how the world will be?
If only we could see.
Full of gadgets, robots and also men,
Computers instead of paper and pen.
Machines and robots to do all your chores,
They'll probably be used to protect the laws.
Mind you, this is only my prediction,
What's your vision?

Daniel Lowe (13)
St Bede's Catholic Grammar School, Bradford

Trees

Their never-ending columns rising into the sky,
The light from the sun,
From the heavens above,
Make the leaves twinkle.

The noises of wildlife,
The owls and the bees,
As you will walk,
Moving swiftly with the trees.

The magnificent, magical colours,
Illuminating the light blue skies.

The old leaves are falling,
The new trees are growing,
So in time,
They can reach up
To the heavens
And be with the others,
To rise up again.

Jacob Muff (13)
St Bede's Catholic Grammar School, Bradford

A Lad Called Matt

There was a lad called Matt
Who often slept on a cat
He ate its fur at night
He had a nightmare, what a fright.

Next night he slept on a dog
He dreamt that he'd been chased by a road hog
He tripped up on a cat
And that was the end of the lad called Matt.

Christopher Hopwood (12)
St Bede's Catholic Grammar School, Bradford

My Mother Needs To Buy Me New Trainers

Toes are scabby
The knuckles are hairy
But what lies beneath
Is even more scary

The inner sole of my trainer
Stinks like my sweat
Turning my new white socks
Into a nasty snotty colour

The overall look
Is such a disgrace
And I think the time has come
To buy a new pair . . . *today!*

Luke Jawnyj (13)
St Bede's Catholic Grammar School, Bradford

Football

A football pitch is big and green
The stands are big, the players look small
When they score you hear a roar
They celebrate and jump for joy

The crowd goes wild in celebration
The coaching staff all so happy
They hope that they can score again
And jump for joy again and again

All the players run around
The referee awards the goal
The other fans, they all boo
And at the end they all feel blue.

Jordan Lightowler (14)
St Bede's Catholic Grammar School, Bradford

Grandma

A character, my gran,
Old-fashioned and dated,
With modern ideas
She's quite belated!

She has her talents
That make me smile,
She loves to spoil me,
Once in a while!

She likes to tell stories
All the time,
But why can't she ever
Hear out mine?

Spending time with her is fine,
Learning all about her past,
But when the time to talk is mine,
She turns her hearing aid off, real fast!

But at the end of the day you see,
With all my heart I love my gran,
Nobody else, only me,
Will always be her biggest fan!

Alex Blaikie (13)
St Bede's Catholic Grammar School, Bradford

The Corridor

Bare, thin and long,
It creaked as loud
As a choir song,
Straight and not proud.

Imperfectly perfect,
The corridor had no bend,
It left a dulling effect
And bang, it hit the end.

David Rossiter (13)
St Bede's Catholic Grammar School, Bradford

Sanjay: Missing Child?

Like a sunflower, tall and strong James stood,
His outfit would hide how he really felt.
These hands full of dirt, a shovel and gloves,
He could not believe it was over.

As he stood above the rancid hole,
Where Sanjay was to lie forever,
The misplaced guilt flooded him,
Like a tidal wave in a hurricane.

How could he have done it?
Sanjay was his friend.
Dearly loved and cared for by many,
How could James face Sanjay's family?

Sanjay's mother's faith would stay alive,
Not definitely dead,
Could he be alive?
For the time to come Sanjay will be reported,
A missing child.

Alex Machen (13)
St Bede's Catholic Grammar School, Bradford

Mixed Seasons

The snow was glistening in the sun,
The snowwoman melting, starting with her bun,
The frozen rain was beginning to go,
But that was the cycle of the white snow,
I wanted it to stay,
When it's gone, where could we play?

The sun's now shining in the sky,
Like a red-hot oven cooking a pie,
There's been no rain for weeks,
I wish I was in the Himalayan mountain peaks,
Even as I sit at the stern,
The sun's rays continue to burn.

James Le Blanc (13)
St Bede's Catholic Grammar School, Bradford

Pilot

Land, cities, towns, fields
Fly
Beneath me
Men have made what ice could not
And ancient shapes are seen
But silent

They hear me first
Bang
And I appear
Then distance spreads between us
And no time to be familiar here

Who am I?
I am unknown
For death and destruction
Is my origin

There is a cold beauty here
Only seen to those like me
Who
Can watch the arc of Earth
Approach
And disappear

Though mortal
I pass through space
Where men and eagles envious of such speed
Can only glimpse
My passing.

Isaac McGladdery (13)
St Bede's Catholic Grammar School, Bradford

Chess - A Battle?

He moves out his triumphant black knight,
Out of its stable onto a white.
Out slides his bishop, wide on the field,
There it stays, as out comes a pawn with sword and shield.
There go the black knights again,
Hoping to devastate and cause some pain.
They join together in the centre of the plain,
Hoping to draw blood once again.
Off they go, taking two - a pawn and a rook,
Before they too must go from an opponent's right hook.
On fight a group of pawns with a rook,
Fighting with great style, skill and luck.
Now into play come the almighty queens,
Aiming for each other, killing by any means.
Casualties taken by each of the teams,
With the white taking the upper hand as it seems.
Fighting carried on all night and into the morn,
Only the king left with a pawn.
On the other hand, however,
The whites have many more,
They say 'cause they were strong and clever.
Later on it came down to the final showdown,
So on ran the queen, her face strewn with a frown.
Out thrust her sword as she slashed at the king,
As she withdrew it, she was aware of the blood
that covered the thing.
The white were victorious as the king slumped to the floor
And the remaining pawn and injured withdrew.

Howard Usher (13)
St Bede's Catholic Grammar School, Bradford

Future

Many futures are yet to be born,
That is for certain.
Many paths lead from here,
That is for certain.
The future is not set,
That is for certain.

Choice is not for certain.
Millions of futures depend on choice.
Millions of paths depend on choice.

Many paths lead from this place,
Only one is for certain.

Choice,
The downfall of the future
And eventually of mankind.

Dominic Makohon-Keogh (13)
St Bede's Catholic Grammar School, Bradford

Sleep

I lie in bed and wonder why,
To fall into the blessed dreams,
Sees peace and rest just disappear,
To me every night sleep only teams
Itself with boredom or with craze.

Strange though it seems to other men,
In a restless time, I venture forth,
In the company of carnivorous fish
And talking squirrels, I prove my worth,
I dream some crazy dreams!

Thomas Crowley (13)
St Bede's Catholic Grammar School, Bradford

Dream

Dream is imagination,
Flowing through the mind,
Thinking different thoughts,
All of the time.

Dream is vision,
Things we're meant to see,
We make it up ourselves,
It's our destiny.

Dream is fantasy,
Nothing that is real,
Just any old thought we think,
It's not even true.

Dream is hallucination,
Like being put under a spell,
See things we normally don't,
What's happening to me?

Dream is what we think, hear and see,
Only when we are asleep.

Christopher Polechonski (13)
St Bede's Catholic Grammar School, Bradford

Noises!

I heard a noise in the night
It was not me and it gave me a fright
I got up and walked around
Then I got back into bed and heard it again.
I looked out the window and saw a hand
It made me jump and came at me fast,
Then I got up and heard a band.

Adam Cooke (13)
St Bede's Catholic Grammar School, Bradford

The Dispirited Nation

Butter fingers James,
Sweating like a fool,
Passes to Rio,
Who acts real cool.

Out wide to Ashley,
Who runs up the wing,
Does one then two,
The crowd begins to sing,
He gets tackled
And wins a throw-in.

Throws it to Gerrard,
Beckham is open,
But gives to Lampard,
Then he gets fouled.
Beckham to take,
It's intercepted,
Zidane goes on a run . . .

He shoots . . .
He scores . . .
We lose . . .
Again.

Ryan Newton (13)
St Bede's Catholic Grammar School, Bradford

The Match

The thrill of a kick
The stamp of a boot
The head of a ball
All while the crowd hoot

The chant of the fans
The score of a goal
The scream of the boss
It's all heart and soul

The referee's whistle
The hails from a fan
The beautiful game
I'll do whatever I can

The skill of Pele
The dive of Pires
With Superman's cape
'Penalty,' he says

The game was a good one
We won 2-1
Now let's all go down the pub
And have some fun.

Jamie Flinn (13)
St Bede's Catholic Grammar School, Bradford

Fear

Fear is something you cannot control,
It is something in your mind, a second voice,
It is your conscience telling you danger is ahead,
Something you have never liked or enjoyed.

Your palms become sweaty
And you begin to shake,
You begin to doubt yourself,
'Is it one big mistake?'

Fear is anxiety, is it right or is it wrong?
It is nerves too big for yourself to control.
That voice that screams at you, 'Don't do it!'
Yet it makes you doubt yourself as a man.

You begin to question your ability.
'Is it going to break?'
Your friends might make fun of you,
So you decide to do it, but it's one big *mistake!*

Ryan Ingham (15)
St Bede's Catholic Grammar School, Bradford

The Heroes Of War

To our heroes of the war,
Who managed to survive the blood and gore,
Fire in the army's heart,
Every man plays a part.

The impact like a Japanese gong,
The pain they suffered will never be gone.

There was weeping,
There was suffering,
There was lightning,
Blood was everywhere,
Yet some remain
And we salute you.

Edward Isaac (13)
St Bede's Catholic Grammar School, Bradford

Remember

Picture the scene. 1945.
November the 11th.
Across fields of trenches and wire
Through streams of bloodshed
Dotted with corpses,
Grows one single, solitary poppy.
A lasting monument to the troops who have fallen.

Forever it will stand upon scarred ground.

Picture the scene. 2001.
September the 11th.
Busy afternoon in Manhattan
Thousands of passers-by
Two towers stood on the skyline of New York
Tall, majestic, picturesque.
Two planes, two minutes, two towers came falling down.
Chaos. Bin Laden had mastered a new rise of terrorism.
For now, where two towers had stood, the ground was at level zero
And it was at ground zero that thousands of wreaths
Were placed in memory
Of the innocents who were slaughtered.

Forever they will stand upon scarred ground.

Joseph Begaj (14)
St Bede's Catholic Grammar School, Bradford

The Weekend

At the weekend I learnt to play,
At the weekend I found new friends,
At the weekend I played all day,
At the weekend I never wanted it to end.

Jack Tallant (13)
St Bede's Catholic Grammar School, Bradford

Remember The Good Times

Remembering. What's the use?
Skies of blue that turn to gold,
I'm only fourteen years old.

Your perfect gaze,
From those dark brown eyes,
A mind of wit and light surprise.

Fifteen years, yet I know you less,
Sahara desert to watercress,
To a different country you've gone.

We're leagues apart,
So far away, incendiary memories,
Your voice in the blaze.

Year sixteen, and now you've come home,
Two long years, I've been alone.
Come to my open arms.

We bide our time and bottle up
Feelings that are solid consoled,
Now we are both getting old.

Sweet seventeen, we are together,
An everlasting promise, broken never,
A golden bond we've tied.

Years pass, people change,
Reaching the Grim Reaper's range,
The raven's salty breath.

So here's our last,
My time has passed,
But we will come again.

Daniel Murgatroyd (14)
St Bede's Catholic Grammar School, Bradford

Remember, Do You?

Do you . . . the last time?
Remember, do you?

Do you remember the last time you laughed?
Do you remember the last time you cried?
Do you remember the last time you smiled?
Do you remember the last time you danced?
Remember, do you?

Could you imagine not laughing?
Could you imagine not crying?
Could you imagine not smiling?
Could you imagine not dancing?
Could you?

Never forget.

Was it yesterday?
Was it last week?
Was it last year?
When was it?

Have you ever laughed?
Have you ever cried?
Have you ever smiled?
Have you ever danced?
Have you?

Do you know anyone that can't laugh?
Do you know anyone that can't cry?
Do you know anyone that can't smile?
Do you know anyone that can't dance?
Because I do.

Leon Flerin (13)
St Bede's Catholic Grammar School, Bradford

Season By Season

Remember.
He wished he could.
The strike left him empty,
A weapon constructed from a piece of wood.

Accomplishing nothing,
Like a hole in his head.
Nothing there,
He wished he was dead.

Everyone was made for a reason.
Time still goes on.
Season by season.
Now he knows it's all in the past,
Something forgotten,
His memory will never last.

Adam Glennon (13)
St Bede's Catholic Grammar School, Bradford

A Certain Poem

I remember a certain poem,
Which threw boredom among people.
Those people liked the colour of rooms.
Pastel shades, crowds, torsos at ease,
In brilliant waters of the warm heart of Africa.

She is the warm heart of Africa
With flowers like towers,
Extreme colours for ordinary situations
For the next generation.

The problem is that the people who know the law,
Won't know of the brilliant flow of waters of the
Warm heart of Africa.

Matthias Chizalema (13)
St Bede's Catholic Grammar School, Bradford

Burnt Hands

Look at the sky.
Look at the smoke.
Look at the fire and sea of faces.
Look at the delight,
All through the night.

If you can see the spark,
In the dark,
All the heart-pumping bangs
And burnt hands.

The way he had to die.
Why?
On top of the fire he burns.
Soon he'll be food for the worms.

Toby Sullivan (13)
St Bede's Catholic Grammar School, Bradford

The Fifth Of November

Fireworks go *bang* and *whizz*,
The bonfire crackles and starts to fizz.
I am standing on the wall,
Trying to see, cos I'm not very tall.

On top of the fire is some guy,
He's burning, I don't care, I'm eating a pie.
The pie burns my mouth, I swallow it quick,
I've eaten too much and now I feel sick.

I have a sparkler, I see a car,
Tomorrow that driver won't get very far.
I light the fuse and push it through the tyre,
Then I run back to the burning bonfire.

Chris Jones (13)
St Bede's Catholic Grammar School, Bradford

1988

Remember, remember
The 5th of November,
1988,
Which might I just add
Is my birth date.
It is also Bonfire Night,
When the sky is so dark,
But then so light.
All the fireworks touching the heart,
Making it look like modern art.

Remember, remember
The 6th of November,
2004,
Where I opened the door
And there were my cards,
They were a day too late,
I'd had to wait
For one more date.
I opened the first and found a fiver,
Opened the second, a picture of a diver.
There was one more.
A piece of white paper fell to the floor.
My heart exploded like a firework.

Francis Barrett (13)
St Bede's Catholic Grammar School, Bradford

Alone

I stand and stare,
I am bare.
The snow is falling
All through the morning.

When I was young,
I was cared for and sprung,
But now I'm tall,
Only squirrels call.

Dogs spring leaks,
I get climbed by freaks.
My branches snap,
My bark cracks.

I remember the days,
When people laid in a haze,
Sat next to me to draw,
Or write or sprawl.

Soon to be a table, a sideboard
Or a chair,
I remember the days,
When people used to care.

Jason Helstrip (13)
St Bede's Catholic Grammar School, Bradford

Always Brings Life

Remember the day when
The day lost its power
When fire struck, buildings
Destroyed and people's tears
Filled the streets, the time
Of flame, anger, destruction.
Here, flowers left
At the evil at hand.

Remember the day when
Night prohibited our country
Black. Black. Black.
When windows stained,
When fear roamed
And tears flowed.
Planes flew and bombs
Dropped.
Fear. Fear. Fear.

Families still visit these
Decaying forces, their
Blood can still be seen
If you look closely
Enough. What can men do
Against such unearthly hate in
The war of all time?
Death. Death. Death.
Always brings life.

Ryan Buckroyd (13)
St Bede's Catholic Grammar School, Bradford

Jibberish

Bored with nothing to do
I got told something to do
But I didn't do it

Bored with something to do
Didn't do it again, why?
Because it was even more boring.

Write this, do that, go there, shut up!
Do this, do that, be quiet, *now!*

Everything needs to be done straight away.

We ask for help - go away
We don't ask for help - why didn't you ask?

Things always go opposite
What am I doing here and why?
Why do we go there? How do aeroplanes fly?

It's a mixed up world with mixed up people
People don't make sense, what's the point?

Arguments turn into riots, destruction of
Nothing, anything, everything

Bored with nothing to do
Maybe I will write some jibberish

No, forget it, I can't be bothered
I'm too bored!

Jason Stockton (14)
St Bede's Catholic Grammar School, Bradford

Football Teams

I really love football
And there are so many teams
There are:
Awesome Arsenal
Brilliant Bolton
Cool Chelsea
Determined Derby
Everlasting Everton
Fantastic Fulham
Intense Ipswich
Loveable Leeds
Magnificent Man U
Notorious Newcastle
Perfect Portsmouth
Skillful Southampton
Wonderful Wolves
But the problem is
Which one to support.

Reece Thomas (13)
St Bede's Catholic Grammar School, Bradford

No Flowers

There were no flowers on his grave,
Just a rotting, chipped, old stone.
I stood there, eyes glazed over,
In the cemetery on my own.

The place in which it laid,
Was fearsome and literally lifeless.
The memories which he left,
Were fading and literally priceless.

Day by day the grave looked older,
When I stood there, with watery eyes.
The grave is still my best mate
And I'm here from sunrise.

Myles Nesbitt (13)
St Bede's Catholic Grammar School, Bradford

Gothic Angel

Beauty of a million angels she possesses,
Gorgeousness too she has been blessed with,
Her eyes, no words can describe how they shine,
When she gazes lovingly back into mine.
Her lips, so soft, so gentle when they touch my skin with a kiss,
And when I hold her in my arms, I feel such indescribable bliss.
I love to hear her gently breathe,
As she lies so silently asleep
And I love to feel her breath
Against my face, like a tender caress.

Antony Cooper (15)
St Bede's Catholic Grammar School, Bradford

Football

I kicked the ball
I kicked it high
It went so high
It touched the sky

It came back down
I had a frown
There was no roar
Because I didn't score.

Stephen Harrison (13)
St Bede's Catholic Grammar School, Bradford

Forgetfulness

I really can't remember what this poem is about.
So if you could, would you take the time to find out?
I would certainly like to know,
I've a few more verses to go.

Now you have told me what I wanted to hear,
I'm off to the pub for a pint of beer.

Chris Mitchell (13)
St Bede's Catholic Grammar School, Bradford

The Wrestler's Poem

And then came on the light,
My opponent was in sight,
He wanted to have a fight,
But all I can do is bite,
He was huge in height,
And he hit me with all his might,
As I came around my bandage was tight,
Instead of swearing I told them to fly a kite,
The nurse was polite,
She attended me all night,
After my unforeseen plight.

Matthew Riley (13)
St Bede's Catholic Grammar School, Bradford

The Daytime Sleep

I'm stuck in here
I'm forced to be here
I have to be here
I need to be here
For me, myself and my future

Sometimes I think - *do I really need this?*
Sat in class fighting the sleep
I just want to close my eyes

I hate being here
I wish anything to be at home
To be with my friends
Messing round and going up to town
I am so bored I just want to sleep

I want to sleep . . .
I have to sleep . . .
I need to sleep . . .
I'm going to sleep.

Paul Bennett (14)
The George Farmer Technology College, Holbeach

Love

Is love just round the corner?
Where do you go?
How do you find it?

Someone falls in love so quickly
Why can't I find it?
Where do you go?
How do you find it?

Trust
A strong feeling inside
I don't have that
Where do you go?
How do you find it?

Maybe my love
Is sitting round the corner
Just waiting to be found
One day perhaps for me
The trust of love I will see.

Laura Goldsmith (14)
The George Farmer Technology College, Holbeach

Flowers

I start as a seed
Farmer sets me in a dark hole
Mud thrown over me
Water stops me breathing.

As I start growing
Taller and taller
My petals start to unfold
I awaken to other flowers.

Am I as tall and bright as them?
Yes, I am like the sun
Big, orange-yellow
A magnificent glow.

Rayner Coole (14)
The George Farmer Technology College, Holbeach

Andrea

Andrea stands in the corner
Fiery-red flows over her gown,
Ralphie, her puppy, whines beside her
As big, clumsy tears tumble down.

The floor is scattered with broken glass
A single white rose at her toes,
What has poor little Andrea seen?
A secret that little girl knows.

Her frock is tattered and shabby
The frills ripped at the seam,
Her knee-high socks have fallen down
Her shoes have lost their gleam.

The floor is scattered with broken glass
A single white rose at her toes,
What has poor little Andrea seen?
A secret that little girl knows.

Andrea's face is unhappy and scared
Her dainty cheeks stained with tears,
Where is the poor child's mother
To hug away all her fears?

The floor is scattered with broken glass
A single white rose at her toes,
What has poor little Andrea seen?
A secret that little girl knows.

Melany Clark (15)
The George Farmer Technology College, Holbeach

The 31st Of October

Witches, wizards, cats and bats!
Cauldrons, spells and pointed hats!
Spooks that haunt creepy habitats.
Hocus, pocus, trick or treat
That's the way witches greet!

Wild witches wearing pointed hats
Pouring potions with black cats!
Cauldrons flowing with green goo.
Who are we cooking?
Guess it's you!

Trick or treaters crawl from Hell,
The sound of cackling,
Ringing the bell.

They've come for us,
Candy and all,
Can they scare us?
Like a ghoul!

Daggers and horns,
Cats and bats,
Round they come,
For midnight snacks.

31st of October,
Demons are unleashed,
Hide away till midnight comes
And life will end In peace.

Amy Wilson (14)
The George Farmer Technology College, Holbeach

Stages Of A Flower

It starts as a seed
Alone, cold and small
It moves to a spot
Alone, cold and small
It grows a shoot
Alone, cold and small

It changes its colours
Satisfied, mutual and tall
It grows some leaves
Satisfied, mutual and tall
It climbs to a height
Satisfied, mutual and tall

It shows a bud
Pretty, happy and flowered
It shows more colours
Pretty, happy and flowered
It grows some petals
Pretty, happy and flowered

It grows more seeds and it starts again.

Kirsty Newby (14)
The George Farmer Technology College, Holbeach

Hallowe'en

Hallowe'en, the spookiest night ever
Anger strikes trick or treaters
When no one answers.
Lots of sweets for all
Laughter and joy from everyone
Owls hooting louder and louder
Witches soaring on their brooms
Every door has been knocked on
End is near
Disappointment on kids' faces
Until next year.

Josh Mann (14)
The George Farmer Technology College, Holbeach

The Disadvantages Of Old Age

I've lived a long life,
Overcome some great tasks,
I've got a wonky hip
And a great osteopath.

No one treats me with respect,
Don't let me in the queue,
But I ram them in the ankles
With my shopping bag and shoes.

My family treats me with respect,
Look after my cat,
But I'm in a care home,
In room 52.

I'm 84 now and getting on a bit,
Here comes the drugs trolley, nurses giving loads of gyp,
My grandchildren come to visit me every other day,
We all laugh and sing, as the children play.

It's not bad here,
I've had a long life,
I am not scared of dying,
So to all a good night.

Steven Wetherell (14)
The George Farmer Technology College, Holbeach

Goodbye Flowers

Flowers small,
Flowers bright,
Flowers sparkling in the dark, cold nights,
Above me in the velvet night sky,
You bring so much joy, you could make people cry,
At night we make special wishes and hope that you hear,
All of our dreams to hold you near,
But now we have to say goodbye,
Because the imperfect dawn is nigh.

Sarah Thwaites (14)
The George Farmer Technology College, Holbeach

Season Flower

Grow and grow is what it does
From just a little seed
To a bright, beautiful flower
Pink and blue, the colour of the petals
Springtime

Time for being picked
Will it get picked, will it not?
No one knows until the farmer comes
Summertime

Leaves start to change colour
Petals begin to plunge
Its head slowly tumbling
Autumn time

The flower almost bare
The head fully drooped
Time for the seeds to spread
At least till next year
Wintertime.

Natasha Frolich (14)
The George Farmer Technology College, Holbeach

Rose

As the garden sparkles after the morning dew
Your petals and arm-like leaves unfold
You stand tall and proud
Recognised for the flower that you really are

The shimmering sun comes out from hiding
And your petals gleam in the rich sunlight
Making everyone around you feel warm and happy

The air soon fills with that wonderful scent
How can anyone resist you?
The beautifully coloured and scented rose.

Clementine Cousins (14)
The George Farmer Technology College, Holbeach

I Saw A . . .

I saw a cloud go eek, eek, eek
I saw a man jump over the moon
I saw a banana as cute as can be
I saw a boy all straight and green
I saw a bus with curly hair
I saw a goat all red with rage
I saw a cherry full of children
I saw a school all blue and green
I saw a car as furry as a bear
I saw a dog with grey and white fur
I saw a cat all strong and tall
I saw a person shutting down
I saw a computer with strange colours
I saw a box all white and round.

Zoie Crowley (14)
The George Farmer Technology College, Holbeach

Sun

The sun is going to get us
Run, run, run
Hide away from the stinging sun
He won't get us

Get in a queue, he won't see us
Run, run, run
Get in a shop or stay undercover
He won't get us

The sun is like a flower, big, bright and colourful
Run, run, run
Like a rainbow showing startling colours
He won't get us.

Andy Dunham (14)
The George Farmer Technology College, Holbeach

Away

We are running away,
They will never get us
Because we are away,
Far, far away.
The horse is running away,
I am running away,
We are running away,
We are running away together.
They will never find us,
The horse and I,
We are out of sight
Because we are running away.
Away from the cities,
Away from the queues,
Away from the crowds.
We are running away,
Through the darkest dark
And the gloomiest gloom,
Through the mist
And through the fog,
Try and get us,
We'll never stop.
Because we are running away,
Far, far away.

Beth Davis (14)
The George Farmer Technology College, Holbeach

Imagination

In the world there is a town,
In that town there is a house,
And at that house there is a garden.

In that garden there is a bush,
On that bush there is a flower,
That flower is a rose.

On this rose there are dashes of pink,
With that pink there is red,
On the red there is a rainbow.

Follow the rainbow down to earth,
On the ground there are the roots,
The roots and gold and sunny.

On the roots there is a pot,
In that pot there is gold,
Glistening like the sun.

In the world there is a town,
In that town there is a house,
At that house there is a garden

At the bottom of the garden,
Lies your imagination . . .

Naomi Stephens (14)
The George Farmer Technology College, Holbeach

Love

Is love just a word,
Or is it a feeling
That comes from inside?
What do you think love is?

Do you think there's more
Than just a mother's love
Forever changing
Or the same throughout life?

Is love given at times
Of need
Or given all year round
No matter what?

To me love is a feeling
That comes from deep inside
That my mum gives me
No matter what.

Jackie Cooke (15)
The George Farmer Technology College, Holbeach

Peter Pumpkin, Pumpkin Pie

Peter Pumpkin, pumpkin pie
When I eat you, you make me cry
When I cry it makes me laugh
Reminds me of my little giraffe
Tipsy, oops a daisy
That's why I'm feeling a little crazy
Crazy girl who eats all day
And dances and smiles along the way
To the pumpkin field where Peter's
Guarding with his shield.

Laura Ashton (14)
The George Farmer Technology College, Holbeach

The King Of The Sky

Crow, crow, of the night,
Your eyes gleaming so, so bright.
Crow, crow, of the night,
Flying around spreading fright.

Crow, crow, of the day,
You spend your time hidden away.
Crow, crow, of the day,
Relying on death to lead your way.

Your job on Earth was to scare away darkness,
But now you've turned out so, so heartless.
Crow, crow, of the world,
Your mission is over, you've been hurled.

Sean Gabriel (12)
The George Farmer Technology College, Holbeach

Fever

Disco fever
Hip hop fever
You've got fever
I've got fever
Limbo fever
Jump up fever
Music fever
Dancing fever
Love is fever
I am fever
Want some fever
Come get fever.

Sam Collins (14)
The George Farmer Technology College, Holbeach

My Dog: A Genius If Only I Could Train Him

A gardener
if only he would dig in the right place
A decorator
if only he wouldn't leave a hairy trace
An umbrella
if only he didn't shake himself all over the floor
A cleaner
if only he didn't eat my socks and shoes and much, much more
A neighbourhood watch
if only he got on with the cat called Bob
A security guard
if only he would stay awake on the job
A doorbell
if only he barked when someone knocked
A genius
if only his talents were unlocked.

Nicholas Mackelden (13)
The George Farmer Technology College, Holbeach

Loving Me For Me

Your lips, your eyes, your smile, your kiss,
I must admit it's a part of me.
You please me, complete me, filling me,
Like a melody.
Your soul, your flow, your youth, your truth,
Is simply proof we were meant to be.
But the best quality that's hooking me,
Is that you're loving me for me.

Emma Frost (14)
The George Farmer Technology College, Holbeach

Remembrance

As I stood on the line with the men,
Ready to go over the top again,
The rain swept from the right,
The misty fog affected their sight.

The guns all cleaned and oiled,
Aimed through the wire all torn and coiled,
Men running in risking their lives,
Leaving their loved ones, even their wives.

Grenades exploded and guns were fired,
These men were brave and should be admired.
When the guns did finally cease,
These men thought they had brought us peace.

Daniel Stanton (15)
The George Farmer Technology College, Holbeach

The Flower

The flower is delicate, like a newborn baby
It starts to bloom in the early spring
The bright and bold colours

Within time the flower grows
It develops new leaves
People adore its bright colours

Eventually the flower will die
Leaving the garden bare during the winter weeks
No pretty flower there to look at
But it'll be back again in the spring.

Amber Rippin (14)
The George Farmer Technology College, Holbeach

My Kittens

I wake up in the morning,
They are there rubbing my face,
I go for a shower,
They are waiting for me,
I go and get dressed,
They are jumping at me,
I go to have breakfast,
They are mauling me,
I do my hair,
They are playing with my clips,
I watch TV,
They cry at me,
I feed them,
They forget me,
I leave for school,
They stare at me,
'It's OK babies, I will be back soon,'
The first thing I say,
At the beginning of the day.

Danielle Coe (15)
The George Farmer Technology College, Holbeach

In A Dark Wood

In a dark, dark wood there was
                a dark, dark house
And in that dark, dark house there was
                a dark, dark room
And in that dark, dark room there was
                a dark, dark cupboard
And in that dark, dark cupboard there was
                a dark, dark shelf
And on that dark, dark shelf there was
                a dark, dark box
And in that dark, dark box there was . . .

Natalie Fensom (14)
The George Farmer Technology College, Holbeach

Dad Has Gone

All we could do was sit and wait,
Mum yelling, Dad at the gate,
Crying, screaming, turning blue,
You would know if it happened to you.

Dad had gone and we were there,
All his cupboards were dark and bare,
Weekend visits for an hour or two,
I hated it and so would you.

Hardly see him anymore,
Five times a year and that's a chore,
No call just to sit and chat,
Believe me we can deal with that.

Now I know what really went on,
I'm not sorry he has gone,
I've added up, done the sum,
I'm better off here with my mum!

Jodie Brogan (14)
The George Farmer Technology College, Holbeach

Pumpkin Face

It has a frightening face,
But has no facial features,
Its skin is smooth,
No hair lies upon its bare head,
It never smiles to welcome,
It scares the most around the time of terror -
Hallowe'en - it never fails to miss,
Everybody wants it around to scare,
Beware of its frightening stare.

Rhea Frederick (13)
The George Farmer Technology College, Holbeach

A Love I Cannot Share

I wasn't supposed to love you,
You are just my friend,
So why do I have these feelings?
I just want them to end.

You do not feel the same way,
I know this for a fact,
But what am I supposed to do,
When these feelings keep coming back?

They do not go away,
No matter how hard I try,
But I simply cannot tell you,
I would rather break down and cry.

So I am stuck with this pointless crush,
This is so unfair,
But I am not able to tell you,
Because your reaction I cannot bear.

No one knows how I feel for you,
And I hope to keep it that way,
Because I think if you found out,
You would just turn and walk away.

Mandy Warren (15)
The George Farmer Technology College, Holbeach

Pumpkins And Cabbages

A big, plump pumpkin,
It's orange and it's round,
They're as bright as marigolds,
The colours are like the sun.

As round as a cabbage,
Inside is like a maze,
You could get lost inside it,
In your big mansion.

Kayleigh Brownsword (13)
The George Farmer Technology College, Holbeach

Happiness

Happiness is like waking up to a bright summer's day,
Scoring a winning goal with the cheer of the crowd beckoning,
It is seeing a hurt child being comforted in the arms of trust.

Happiness is like finding the pot of gold at the end of the rainbow,
Opening the gift you have been waiting for your whole life,
It is finding out you are in love with that certain person.

Happiness is like knowing you are in good health,
Being surrounded by the people you love,
It is seeing your friends and family enjoying life and one another.

Happiness is like getting the job of your dreams,
Winning the million pounds lottery,
A brand new life being brought into the world,
It is finding the end line to the poem you are writing.

Nicola Bullock (15)
The George Farmer Technology College, Holbeach

English War Poem

War was a joke to me and you
I soon learnt my dreams weren't true.
I heard an army charging upon the land
The orders came, we were told to stand.

After a while there were no more bombs of ours or theirs
Silence as every man stood and stared.
The battle was over, time now to bring in
Reinforcements and get our guns repaired.

After the blast from the east
After all the guns had ceased
Every man had hoped he'd brought peace.

Darren Taylor (15)
The George Farmer Technology College, Holbeach

Hello Mr Moon

Hello Mr Moon
What are you doing
Shining so bright
In the night sky?

Hello Mr Moon
How are you doing?
It must be cold
Up in the dark sky.

Hello Mr Moon
What is it like when you leave?
Is it sad
Or is it happy?

Hello Mr Moon
Is it nice when you're back?
It certainly is
For me.

Duncan Cooke (14)
The George Farmer Technology College, Holbeach

Autumn

The sun is shining,
The birds are singing,
The leaves are red,
It's autumn!

The wind is strong,
The gloves come out,
The hat goes on,
It's autumn!

The raindrops fall,
The flowers die,
So many colours,
It's autumn!

José Johnson (15)
The George Farmer Technology College, Holbeach

We Had It Bad

A hundred foot wall stood between us
I wanted him bad
The hurdle was there

I wanted his eyes
I wanted his nose
Most of all, I wanted his heart

As I saw him, I became a dove
A dove soaring around the world
Wanting to find his love for me

I wanted him to be mine

I wanted him so bad
I ran to jump that hurdle
I heard his voice in my head
His voice saying he'd been looking for my love

I cleared that hurdle

I found his love
He found my love

We had it bad!

Emma Inglis (14)
The George Farmer Technology College, Holbeach

Dreams

When I rest my head at night,
I close my eyes and see what went by.

My mind drifts away to another land,
Roaming around in the sand.

Seeing stars and rainbows,
Great big giants and pink flamingos.

Your dream is over,
It's time to wake,
Let's hope it comes back with a great big cake!

Stacey Doades (15)
The George Farmer Technology College, Holbeach

Lost And Found

This morning, my mum reminded me
To check the 'lost and found'.
So just to make her happy,
I took a look around.

There was a box like a mouldy fridge,
Whose grin was dark and wide,
I gulped and took a huge breath,
Then reached my arm inside.

I dug around without a sound,
Through swirls of clothes and dirt,
To my delight the box spat out,
My favourite red shirt.

I dug a little deeper down
And there, to my surprise,
A little face gazed up at me,
With wide and poorly eyes.

I took another look
And saw it was my sister,
It's sad to think, for several weeks,
We hadn't even missed her.

Lindsay Graham (14)
The George Farmer Technology College, Holbeach

The Rock

A rock blocks the path.
Blocks the way.
Nothing can get by.
There's no way round.
No way to the other side,
The other side of the rock.

Ben Flowers (14)
The George Farmer Technology College, Holbeach

Football Madness

Ball is laid
On the ground
One team starts
Then they frown
Pass it once, twice,
Three times again
Then they score
Four minutes into the game
Forty-five minutes comes
Half-time
Have a rest
For some time
Second half has to start
No more goals till the end
Doesn't matter, one team won
End of the game
Now I head home.

Kyle Rackham (14)
The George Farmer Technology College, Holbeach

What's Under Your Bed?

What's under your bed? Nobody knows.
Some leftover food, some screwed up clothes?
A rotten smell or hairball fluff?
Will you take a peek, will you take a look?

What's under your bed? Will you clear it up?
Is it stuck to the carpet, is it stuck to the rug?
Is it dried on or fresh, will you touch it and see?
Have I lost it ages ago, did it once belong to me?

What's under your bed? It's moving around.
An alive, smelly pile, a stinking old mound?
It's not coming out, it's stuck there for good,
So leave it there settled, I think that you should.

Adam Stacey (14)
The George Farmer Technology College, Holbeach

Love - Is It The Way It Should Be?

Love is something no one can see,
Love is something that no one wants to play with,
If people decide to play with it,
They only get hurt in the process,
Is it the way it should be?

If only love can find us all,
If only hearts didn't have to fall,
We can't mislead to make things right,
Some people are living without love tonight,
Is it the way it should be?

People think they want love,
But they only want it because they never had it,
Love is a complicated thing,
So wait for love to come to you,
Is it the way it should be?

When love doesn't work out,
All you get is 'sorry',
But you lose your temper and lose more
And friends are only trying to help,
Is it the way it should be?

But all you have got to think,
Is that love will find you,
So all you can do is be patient
And hope that it will come to you,
That's the way it should be!

Most people have found their love,
And they are happy in every single way,
Soon I hope to find that love,
I pray that it will stay,
That's the way it should be . . . for all of us!

Lee Lashmar (14)
The George Farmer Technology College, Holbeach

So I Wait

So I stand and wait for you,
Sometimes for hours on end.
Hours turn into days, days turn into months, months turn into years,
But, I don't care,
I'll carry on waiting.

Why I wait for you I'll never know,
But still, I carry on waiting,
For hours, days, months,
Years.

Then I get angry.
You're not here,
You should be,
Why aren't you here?
Then I get sad.
I break down,
Fall onto my knees,
Burst into tears.
Then I realise
You're not here.

So?
Why does that matter?
I can wait.
You'll be back.
Don't know when,
Don't know where,
But you'll be back.
And I'll be waiting for you.
Always.
Forever.

Edward Carfrae (14)
The George Farmer Technology College, Holbeach

Why?

One more innocent person
Killed by a bullet
One more life taken
By the gun in your hands
One more family destroyed
By the pain of loss
Why?
Just another day in the torture of war.

One more life deleted
Instead of saved
One more child hurt
Instead of held
One more mother crying
Instead of smiling
Why?
Just another day in the torture of war.

Why trap someone
When you can free someone?
Why damage someone
When you can repair someone?
Why ignore someone
When you can help someone?
Why do anything
But love someone?

Chamise Nocera (14)
The George Farmer Technology College, Holbeach

What A Dog

Once I had a dog
Who I took for a jog
Every time we ran
It made him pant
Until one day
He ran away, never to pant again.

Joanne Bradley (13)
The George Farmer Technology College, Holbeach

Tennis Balls

Tennis balls flying all around
Angry tennis stars shout out loud
The crack of racket
The roars of the crowd
Sighs, roars and groans

Tennis balls flying all around
Rackets hitting the tennis balls
Serve after serve, ace after ace
Don't get behind the pace
Crowd goes wild, shouting in the opponent's face

Tennis balls flying all around
Tension building, silent all around
Throws the ball up, smash
Bounces once, bounces twice, ace
Match point, crowd silent, serve tension building point,
Game, set, match

Tennis balls flying all around
Rackets hitting the tennis balls
Serve after serve, ace after ace
Don't get behind the pace
Crowd goes wild, shouting in the opponent's face.

Luke Hull (14)
The George Farmer Technology College, Holbeach

Weather

The sun is getting warmer
The plants are starting to grow
The days are getting longer
The buds on the trees are beginning to show.

The children are out playing
With bats, balls and skipping ropes
Mums and dads always end up paying
For the ice cream around their chops.

Scott Goodale (13)
The George Farmer Technology College, Holbeach

Holbeach

As I turn the corner
I see rich solicitors
Driving their Jags down the road
In that part of Holbeach

As I turn the corner
And walk down a dark alleyway
I see graffiti sprayed on the wall
In that part of Holbeach

As I walk through town
I see old ladies with shopping trolleys
Who have just been to the Co-op
In that part of Holbeach

As I walk through town
I see builders who have just finished work
Eating fish and chips
In that part of Holbeach.

Daniel Rulewski (14)
The George Farmer Technology College, Holbeach

Dad

Dad, Dad loves me lots
Dad, Dad washes the pots
Dad, Dad says hello
Dad, Dad loves me so.

Dad loves me in the morning
Dad loves me at night
When I go off to school
He gives me a hug real tight.

And now I come to my last verse
I hope he won't be glum
For it isn't really my dad
It's my mum! Mum! Mum!

Ricky Bramley (14)
The George Farmer Technology College, Holbeach

The Following

As I walk, I keep on thinking,
Is it there or is it not?
I look over here,
I look over there,
I just can't seem to grasp it.

As I walk, I keep on looking,
I check over my shoulder,
Every minute, every two, every three.
I walk through the trees, watching my step,
Making sure not to trip, that's when it might strike.

As I walk, I keep getting more nervous,
The sounds behind me are getting louder.
I can't describe the sounds I'm hearing,
A sharp sound behind, sends me to the floor,
Then everything around me is silent.

Daniel Taylor (14)
The George Farmer Technology College, Holbeach

Death

Death is stealthy,
He sneaks up on his prey
And consumes it,
In a huge, black void.

He wears long, black robes,
His face is always hidden,
To hide himself from being seen.

He moves like a lion,
Pouncing on unsuspecting victims,
Swiftly, silently.

Next time you go out,
Watch out,
As Death is always about.

Mark Wright (14)
The George Farmer Technology College, Holbeach

Motors Everywhere

I looked as I walked in,
It was all so bright,
Coventry Transport Museum,
All in the light.

I saw Lara Croft's Land Rover,
And James Bond's Jag,
I nearly fell over,
When I saw the price tag!

I could hear lots of people talking,
The Thrust SSC simulator was loud,
I could hear walking,
The simulator drew the crowd.

As I walked in the simulator,
It started up,
The faster it got,
I nearly threw up.

As I was walking round,
I touched the ground,
I also touched the Thrust SSC,
And a rally car with 450 bhp.

I could taste the air,
We had lunch when we were there,
I had a cream scone,
It wasn't very long till it was gone.

I could smell the lunch,
It smelled good,
I could smell car polish
And that wasn't so good.

Matt O'Leary (12)
The George Farmer Technology College, Holbeach

The Slender Heron

Still, still, still, still
Never moving
Still, still

Waiting for his meal of fish
The greatest angler of them all
As scraggy as an old T-shirt
Which has lost all its colour
In all the years of rain and snow

Still, still, still, still
Never moving
Still, still

When he moves, which is very rare
He struts with his lanky legs
When he flies, which he rarely does
He looks like a prehistoric bird
His slow, relaxed hovering
Makes him look very wise

Still, still, still, still
Never moving
Still, still

The most patient bird in the land
Waiting all day for the tiniest fish
But he's never disappointed
With his proud catch

Still, still, still, still
Never moving
Still, still.

Douglas Mitchell (14)
The George Farmer Technology College, Holbeach

I Am Free

I am one of them
Wild and free
Galloping through the meadow
Following me.
Then I was caught
A rope around my neck
Pulling my legs
'Help!' Is what I said
And then there he was
A stallion
A mighty stallion he was.
Kicking, bucking. Those stupid Italians.
Then I was free
Galloping, I looked back and
There he was, the stallion
Following me.

Emma Tierney (13)
The George Farmer Technology College, Holbeach

The Snow

The snow
Falling on the ground
Creating a soft white blanket
Upon the road.

The snow
Falling on the ground
Creating a soft white blanket
For children to play on.

Rachel Kirk (13)
The George Farmer Technology College, Holbeach

Teachers And Parents

Teachers are like parents
Always telling me what to do
'Tuck your tie in'
'Clean your bedroom'
'Feet off the chairs'
'Shoes off the wall'

What if I told them what to do?
'Don't pick your nose'
'Don't dress like that'
'Don't slurp your coffee'
'Don't be so nosey'

Oh just wait until I am an adult
I'll show them who the boss is!

Lucia Harness (13)
The George Farmer Technology College, Holbeach

Pumpkin

Orange-faced figure,
Looking at me,
Waiting to jump out,
As he sits in the corner.

Decorated with lights,
He silently cries,
As he is alone,
On this dark and scary night.

In the future,
He will burn,
But until then,
He waits for the clock to turn.

Francesca Fowler (13)
The George Farmer Technology College, Holbeach

The Pumpkin

Pumpkins glow orange.
They can be creepy
Once their face is empty.
You cut their skin
Make them hollow.
Put a light in
And make them glow!

You put them out at Hallowe'en.
Some people make a scene
You try your hardest
To make them evil.
When you look at them
They can make you evil.

With the inside of him
You can make some soup.
Make sure you don't
Forget the seeds.
Just check he doesn't mind
His insides going in mine.

Laura Pearl (14)
The George Farmer Technology College, Holbeach

Pumpkin

The orange ball-shaped vegetable.
Scary but nice.
With its orange skin
And its stringy filling.
Its scary face
And the candle in the middle.
They will scare the wits
Out of the witches and ghouls.

Philip Teague (13)
The George Farmer Technology College, Holbeach

Pumpkin's Eyes

Pumpkins lighting up the dusty road
As the children dress up in their clothes
Out comes the pumpkin's glow.

The pumpkins on the road,
Their eyes like the headlights on a car,
Fiery eyes on the pumpkin watch the children
Like smudged faces with
No eyes but an orange face.

With their deep round looking eyes
The light inside the pumpkin goes out
Looking like a long dark alley with no end.

Joshua Wells (13)
The George Farmer Technology College, Holbeach

The Pumpkin

The pumpkin has a wrinkly face
It's like the face of a withered old man
It glows a bright orange
Like a street lamp
Or even the sun
On a hot summer's day

Its green handle
High and proud
But I wonder what's lurking
Underneath the shell,
Light or dark?
Good or bad?

James Waters (13)
The George Farmer Technology College, Holbeach

Pumpkin Poem

Pumpkins are orange
Scary on Hallowe'en
Wait 'til night to give you a fright
With their faces so big and bright
You put a candle in
Light me up
Then you should get a fright
How would you react
If your guts were taken out?
That's what happens to the pumpkin.

Ella Berrie (13)
The George Farmer Technology College, Holbeach

Pumpkins

Pumpkins are big, orange and usually round
Grow up from the muddy ground
When they are cut they are left to dry
We use the pulp to make pumpkin pie
In the outer shell we cut a scary face
For scaring people on the day!

Karl Barfoot (13)
The George Farmer Technology College, Holbeach

Pumpkins

It watches you as you walk by
With your big bag of candy
His glowing evil eyes follow you
Down the long black street
Until the morning comes
When his evil runs out
Till next year.

Jack Putterill (13)
The George Farmer Technology College, Holbeach

It's Back To School

S adness, gladness, happiness are all the emotions.
E verybody booing, some kids cheering, it's back to school.
N early there, first period, hooray it's maths.
S oftness, kindness, everybody happy.
E nd of the day, it went so fast, some kids hooraying but
  I am booing.
S illiness, stupidness, kids are getting detentions already.

Ricky Crane (12)
The George Farmer Technology College, Holbeach

Pumpkins

The orange of evil
Makes the pumpkin rough
It's fat and distorted
As it sits with boredom.
It sits and waits with freedom
As it releases its evil on the night.

Brendan Strowlger (13)
The George Farmer Technology College, Holbeach

A Pumpkin

A pumpkin lay on someone's grass,
Lights glaring out into the eyes,
It is so bright it lights up the night,
Especially on Hallowe'en,
Next year,
The orange thing will burn again,
It just has to wait for the clock to turn.

Cameron Flowers (13)
The George Farmer Technology College, Holbeach

Pumpkin!

The strange, mysterious colour orange;
As deep as blazing fire,
Which is the deep shocking red;
Also shows the compassion that is hot.

Like a container of Hallowe'en;
Evil is ready for an outbreak,
As black as someone's heart;
A mega dark portal for us to enter.

As small as your evil heart;
A holder for the light of worlds,
Like a perfect orange heart;
But a rough surface to touch.

Kevin Hall (13)
The George Farmer Technology College, Holbeach

Pumpkin

Pumpkins look so grumpy
Gazing into the night.
Especially at Hallowe'en
When they are spooky.
It's like an orange ghost
Head with no features.
They're like obese faces
Just looking into the sky at night.

Waiting and waiting for you
To pick them up.
And to jump out at you.
How much would you react to a pumpkin?
In the spooky night sky.

Michelle Cook (13)
The George Farmer Technology College, Holbeach

Pumpkin

October is a fun time of year where we have pumpkins.
Pumpkins are good for two things
One is for growing
Two is you can eat them at Hallowe'en.

A pumpkin is a strange funny shape
I wonder what's inside it?
It is an evil thing at Hallowe'en
Evil eyes and a cheesy smile.

What's inside that orange ball?
Magic or mayhem maybe
That orange ball is such a mystery.

When you're out on Hallowe'en
All you see is pumpkins grinning
With a flicker of light beside them
Pumpkins!
I wouldn't trust them.

William Chenery (13)
The George Farmer Technology College, Holbeach

Salty The Kitten

I found a little kitten
On a summer's day
She was so small and pretty
I asked my mum if she could stay
Where she came from we will never know
She brought such happiness in a short time
We thought she must have been poorly
Her mother must have known
Now she has gone forever
And all I have left
Are memories and photos
And a cross in the garden
Which marks her last resting place.

Charlotte Bacon (12)
The George Farmer Technology College, Holbeach

Cornwall

Cornwall is oh so peaceful,
It's famous for many things.
The sea is always blue,
You can see right to the bottom!
The ice cream is oh so nice,
The clotted cream is oh so nice too!
Everyone seemed to have a smile,
Even my brother!
The Eden Project was nearby,
So too was Merlin's Magical Maze.
You could go horse riding and swimming.
Even visit a brewery.
We had jam and clotted cream scones,
Ice cream too.
I don't think anybody would ever want to leave.
But sadly we had to.
Oh!

Charlotte Booth (12)
The George Farmer Technology College, Holbeach

I Couldn't Believe My Eyes . . .

When I saw my brother . . .
I felt warm, safe and happy.
The noise around me went quiet.
All of a sudden, I ran and cuddled him with a cheer
I had tears in my eyes.

I couldn't believe my eyes . . .
The smell was faint.
I heard a flock of birds chirping.
The wind was carefully swaying in the trees.
I stood there crouched on my knees.

I couldn't believe my eyes . . .
Where I was at that time . . .

Jade Wells (12)
The George Farmer Technology College, Holbeach

The Blue Chip Final

The lorry was full,
The ponies were in and off we went,
The show that night was great,
My cousin jumped in the big class.

Then came my turn,
In the ring I went,
Jumped a great round,
Then came the claps and cheers.

The next minute, in the ring I went again,
With me up the front,
I had won!
That day I will never forget.
But the real star was Garfield my pony.

Sam Spencer (12)
The George Farmer Technology College, Holbeach

Hospital

Back to the hospital again,
With all the bouncy beds,
And the dolls' house in the playroom,
With all these poorly heads.

The cabinet smells like medicine,
The kitchen smells of food,
And down it goes, every sip,
I'd hate to be so rude.

Now that it's all over,
My head still feels so sore.
'Let's go home,' I said to my mum,
Just as I left through the door.

Laura Thompson (12)
The George Farmer Technology College, Holbeach

The Day I Went To See My Friends

The day I went to see my friends,
Was a couple of months ago inside Talkey,
They have blonde hair,
With pale eyes,
And a warm smile.

When I went in,
I heard the laughter and screams,
Of my mum and her friend,
And the talking of me and my friends,
It was a great first meeting.

After all this we all hugged,
And I felt their smooth clothes,
As I walked forward I could smell the smelly food,
Just waiting for us.

My mouth went watery,
I tasted the tasty food,
And felt it trickle down my throat.

I felt so happy those few days
And wished that I could have stayed longer.

Leanne Frith-Anderson (12)
The George Farmer Technology College, Holbeach

Who Is It?

Green grass, grey concrete.
The smell of cooking burgers.
Loads of fun and strange stalls.
Wind in the trees.
Feet on the ground.
Happiness in meeting an old friend.

Daniel Meadows (12)
The George Farmer Technology College, Holbeach

The Long Ride

All I can see is the top of roofs,
The gleaming skies.
I'm seeing the top of the world and the blue seas,
And the people who look like small ants.
Who are crawling all around.
I can see the red rolling track pulling us up as we swirl around.

I can hear the screaming of children and adults
And everyone out of breath but trying to get it back.
All the amusements singing in the background
And my favourite soundtracks.

I can smell the sweet smell of the doughnuts filled with jam,
The sizzling burger all hot with the smelly cheese,
The strawberry candyfloss swirling all in the air
and the longing smell of the hotdogs.

I'm touching the salty arms which is keeping me in my seat
I'm clinging onto my jeans as I go upside down, hoping not to fall out.
I am sucking onto my humbug hoping not to choke.
It is really tasty,
Ahh! it is stopping. *Never again!*

Craig Cumberworth (12)
The George Farmer Technology College, Holbeach

Spain

Ice cream, ice cream everywhere,
Seagulls flying in the air
Warm seawater, fish to see
People having fun with me.
Ice cream, ice cream everywhere,
Seagulls flying in the air
Warm seawater, fish to see
People having fun with me.

Adam Smith (12)
The George Farmer Technology College, Holbeach

When I Met A Dragon

I looked out of my window
And guess what I saw?
A dragon flying high in the sky
I gazed at the sky
Full of fear and excitement.

When the green slimy head looked down,
It stared through my window at me,
It was outside my window,
Fire-breathing, human-seeking dragon,
Looking at me.
Oh, what a day!

It punched the window with his fist,
The window shattered to pieces,
He poked through the empty space,
Sarcasm filled the room as he said, 'Hello!'
I screamed and darted to the kitchen,
Mum and I entered the room,
And the dragon I saw . . .

Had disappeared.

Barbara Bearman (11)
The George Farmer Technology College, Holbeach

Going Home From School

The air as sweet as sugar
The trees blowing in the breeze

The kids are out playing
The trees are all swaying

The cars are driving, driving, gone
The cool calm breeze

A dog with lots of fleas.

Jack Robinson (12)
The George Farmer Technology College, Holbeach

Boxes

Boxes, boxes, boxes
Everywhere boxes
Moving boxes
Package boxes
Always boxes
Boxes, boxes, boxes.

I like boxes
I hate boxes
I squash boxes
I burn boxes
Everywhere boxes,
Boxes, boxes, boxes.

Big box
Little box
Cardboard box
Squashed box
Neat box
Everywhere is *boxes!*

Zac Rowlett (12)
The George Farmer Technology College, Holbeach

Holidays

H appy, no more school
O n the PlayStation 2 I played
L azy all day
I   stayed in the lounge
D ay by day
A gain and again
Y es, longer in bed
S ix weeks of boring time.

Sam Feetham (12)
The George Farmer Technology College, Holbeach

My Life Story

I've had a hard time in my life,
It's like I've been stabbed with a knife,
Whenever I feel the drop of a tear,
It feels like I've been hit with fear.

I want the past to disappear,
And I want the future to come near,
I just want to live with my mum or my dad,
Because I feel ever so sad.

It seems like my life's been taken away,
It's like I've just got to stay,
A chunk of my life's just been lost,
Just like the morning and the frost.

I wish it could float into the sky,
Then it could float just right by.
They're too far to touch but way too near,
It seems like they're waiting till I get out of here!

AJ O'Connor (11)
The George Farmer Technology College, Holbeach

The Flower Of Imagination

The flower of imagination
Stays beside the magic waterfall.
There is only one kind of this flower,
And it's behind an invisible wall!

Pink and purple
With a stem so long.
If you go near it,
It will burst into song!

I found this flower,
And it's my creation.
It stays beside the waterfall,
The flower of imagination!

Gemma Whincup (11)
The George Farmer Technology College, Holbeach

What Is A Laugh?

People say that laugher
Is the best medicine of all.
We sometimes laugh at pain or fear
Or sometimes even laugh at ourselves
In home videos.
We laugh at different situations
People in a struggle.
We laugh when other people laugh
Contagious is what it is.
We laugh at different things
Like rude remarks, nature or things we see on TV.

We have different types of laughs
Like Santa, evil geniuses or giggles maybe.
You laugh when you're embarrassed
You laugh at a good old joke.
I think comedians are the best
They have a power like no other
They have the power to make you well
They have the power to make your day complete.

What is a laugh?
The best thing you could possibly have!

Allan Taylor (12)
The George Farmer Technology College, Holbeach

A Gleaming Daffodil

Golden daffodil
Gleaming in the sun
Blow your golden trumpets
Like a shining sun.

Bloom and be pretty
Show off your yellow beauty
Be tall and elegant
Like a singing lady.

Holly Scott (11)
The George Farmer Technology College, Holbeach

Night Fire

Night-time in the woods,
Animals stare at the coal-black sky
Without a single star glittering,
The night has hidden the sun.

Dark time in the woods,
But a light suddenly flashes
Then starts to grow quickly,
What is it?

Fear time in the woods,
A red, gold and orange flame attacks
Gobbling up ancient trees,
A starving, roaring monster.

Fleeing animals in the woods,
Magpies and owls abandon their nests
The deer gallops away from her grazing,
Because the grass won't be there soon.

Animals searching in the woods,
For the lovely, cool stream
So they will be safe from the burning,
Of the wild fiery beast.

Night fire in the woods,
The animals will come back
Destroyed the old woods,
New woods have risen.

Holly Davis (11)
The George Farmer Technology College, Holbeach

Dolphins

Dolphins are wonderful and glorious things,
All sorts of dolphins,
With a shade of blue.
Some white, some grey,
They're Man's most understanding creatures,
In the entire animal world.

Leap out of the sea,
With a ray of delight,
Singing their dolphin songs,
In the dark of the night gleam,
In the undersea world.
Their big blue shiny eyes,
Their swishing tails
Like an aerobics class
Show all their great abilities.

Jodie Wells (11)
The George Farmer Technology College, Holbeach

Spring

The coming of the warm sun
Brings forth, from the dark earth,
Shoots of emerald green
Long and slender with golden bells
That seem to ring out to me.

Now you know spring is here
When birds seem to be everywhere.
A time for new life to begin.

Zoe Yorke (11)
The George Farmer Technology College, Holbeach

Hallowe'en

Is it spooky?
Is it scary?
Maybe frightening!
What about nasty?
Do you dare?

Ghost and zombies
Witches and vampires
Ghouls and goblins.

Is it nice?
Is it cool?
Maybe friendly!
What about you?
Not really!
But think, it's true!

Sian Hardy-Usher (11)
The George Farmer Technology College, Holbeach

A Bee

A big fat bumblebee
Is chasing me,
I don't know why
I just can't see.

Why oh why must it be me
With all these people he can see?
Why can't it see
I'm not full of pollen for its tea?

Now this bee has gone away
It's near the end of May
He doesn't want to get burned
Thank God the sting has turned.

Ryan Isaacs (11)
The George Farmer Technology College, Holbeach

Dragon

Down in the depths of my garden
There's a dragon sleeping there,
And he's always snoring like a bear.

I tiptoed up to my dragon's cave
He did nothing so I called his name,
Even then he didn't answer
I thought *such a shame.*

'Mum, why doesn't my dragon answer his name?'
She didn't answer, so I asked once again.

She said, 'He can't answer his name,
So stop playing your little game!'
Grown-ups are such a bore
But I know my dragon's real
I heard him snore!

Ben Brunton (11)
The George Farmer Technology College, Holbeach

Starting George Farmer

G reat big year elevens
E verybody rushing,
O pening doors,
R eading books,
G igantic PE teachers,
E veryone talking.

F ighting,
A rms connecting,
R unning to each lesson,
M usic lessons
E lephants stomping down the corridors,
R eaching and stretching.

Emma Woods (11)
The George Farmer Technology College, Holbeach

Lazy Me

My teacher said, 'Write a poem,'
I really couldn't be bothered,
So I did the rest of my homework,
And left this bit till last.

And then it came to English,
I really couldn't think,
So I went to the kitchen,
And poured myself a drink.

I walked into the front room,
And sat in front of the TV,
And thought *I know,*
I'll write a poem about how lazy I could be!

Do you think
There's someone as lazy as me?
I can't be bothered to do anymore,
I want to watch TV.

Chelsey Johnson (11)
The George Farmer Technology College, Holbeach

The Gentlemen's Game

Bone-crunching tackles
And lightning pace
Bring claps of thunder, from the fans
Both teams desperate to win.

Bulging heads contest the scrum
Desperately trying to rake the ball
Slowly to their scrum-half,
As they push it to their hearts' content.

As one team score a try
The opposing team look in despair
Where did they go wrong?
They don't know where!

Jack Beavis (12)
The George Farmer Technology College, Holbeach

Sport

Sport is fun,
It's so great,
Nothing can beat it,
Playing sport,
All day long,
It is so amazing,
Football and tennis,
Badminton too,
Loads of sport,
That you can do,
If you're active,
Then why not do some sport,
Maybe hockey, maybe not,
Maybe you like rugby,
So much sport,
That you can do,
So if you're energetic,
Then why not join in too!

Joshua Smith (12)
The Robert Manning Technology College, Bourne

Tia My Kitten

Tia is a lovely kitten
She bounces all around
She jumps and skips and hops and leaps
But very rarely calms down.

She's soft and fluffy and loving too
But still springs around like a kangaroo
Except when she's tired she purrs and purrs
She snuggles up, it's so absurd.

As she grows she'll roam about and bring us lots of presents
We hope she'll only bring us mice
And not a load of pheasants.

Callum Perry (11)
The Robert Manning Technology College, Bourne

The Match

Saturday's here at last,
The game is about to start,
Man U are ready and Liverpool are in fear,
If Man U lose there will be a tear,
The whistle blows, the match begins,
Man U attack and hit the post,
Dudek, Liverpool's keeper, was lucky there,
Kicks the ball out, hits Ferdinand, falls to Owen, oh no! One-nil.

Straight from the kick-off, Man U reply,
Van Nistelrooy passes to Becks, oh yes! One-all.
Liverpool are rocking 'cause Ronaldo's coming on,
He goes past them all, like there's no one there,
He goes past Dudek like a rocket, puts it in, two-one, Man U.
Five minutes to go and I'm starting to shake,
Liverpool are giving it their all.
The ref looks down at his watch, whistle in mouth, ready to blow,
Half a minute left, they've hit the post we were lucky there,
But we're the team with the most.
The whistle blows, all the Man U fans cheer,
The worrying is over and that's all we need to hear.

Nicholas Pope (11)
The Robert Manning Technology College, Bourne

Spalding

S palding is a small town,
P recious in many ways,
A lso, it's got a few attractions,
L ike Ayscoughfee Gardens and so on,
D own between two roads is the River Welland,
I n Spalding there are all sorts of things but . . .
N ot cathedrals or amusements parks etc. sadly
G ood place I suppose, let's hear your comments.

Mark Saint (11)
The Robert Manning Technology College, Bourne

The Rain

As the clouds gather in the sky
And as I watch, life passes by
It gets darker and muggier
Then it starts to fall.

I feel a trickle on my skin
Then I know it's starting to begin
It hits my skin like a needle on a thorn bush
It's like it has come from nowhere.

The rain is now falling
My heart skips a beat
Now I jump to my feet
No longer can I watch the world pass by
Now I feel it is time to fly.

The rain is colourless
But so powerful
But it makes the whole place dull.

Just as quick as I am inside
The rain has gone.
It looks like it never happened
But life still goes on till next time.

Chloe Temple (11)
The Robert Manning Technology College, Bourne

Bonfire Night

Firework displays
Sparklers sparkling

Bang after bang
Colour after colour

Noise coming from every direction
These are the things that happen on bonfire night!

Amy Laidlow (11)
The Robert Manning Technology College, Bourne

My Teacher

My teacher once wore nappies
My teacher used to crawl
My teacher used to cry at night
My teacher used to bawl.

My teacher used 'jibber jabber'
My teacher ran up stairs
My teacher wrote in squiggles
My teacher stood on stairs.

My teacher once was naughty
My teacher was so rude
My teacher used a bad word
My teacher spilled her food.

My teacher lost her homework
My teacher took too long
My teacher did things wrong.

My teacher's all grown up now
My teacher can't recall
My teacher thinks she's different
My teacher's not at all.

Natalie Fitzjohn (11)
The Robert Manning Technology College, Bourne

The Cat

The cat is black and it wears a hat
It prowls the street for bits of scrap.
Its claws are long and its teeth are sharp.
It eats mice,
It burrows in the bins looking for tins filled with carp.
It smells quite bad,
It gets worse as you burrow deeper into its fur full of dirt.
It sleeps in bundles and bundles of hay
Though you just can't blame it, because it's a stray.

Bethan Dyer (11)
The Robert Manning Technology College, Bourne

My Pub

I live in a pub,
Where they serve good grub,
And the customers like the beer.

They think it is great,
There is nothing they hate,
And everywhere else is dear.

A whiskey, a cider,
A gin or two.
Nothing could work,
Without me and you.

If you feel like singing,
Then come to us.
We can make you happy,
In just one buzz.

So now you know about my home,
If you ever want some food or fun.
Remember just call us on the phone.

Jessica Warburton (11)
The Robert Manning Technology College, Bourne

Football

Football is the beautiful game
All footballers want fame.
But some of them are lame
But could it be your game?
Skills or not
Good or bad
You can still play the beautiful game.

If you train, you will get better.
If you don't, you will get worse.
If you pass the ball, you will score a goal!
Rich or poor, you can still play the beautiful game.

Nicholas Garland (11)
The Robert Manning Technology College, Bourne

Pets

My pet's name is 'Sandy'
She's very lazy
She likes to play
But especially likes to sunbathe.

She's very noisy
Even though she's a softy.
She shares her hutch
But doesn't like it much.

She shares her food with Sophie,
They look very cosy, but look a bit dozy.
She tosses their food in the air
But she doesn't care.
She's a lion-head rabbit.
She's called that because she has a mane,
Her fur colour is sandy
That's why she is called
Sandy.

Catherine Twaite (11)
The Robert Manning Technology College, Bourne

Football

Football is a great sport.
It has so many rules.
Referees and linesmen.
Make sure it's fair.
They sometimes make mistakes.
Like players do themselves.
Smoking and taking drugs.
It's pointless in the end.
Confidence and passion could win you the game.
Blunders and bad challenges and the game is lost.
The crowd cheer and scream.
When the game is up, who will have the last laugh?

James Smith (11)
The Robert Manning Technology College, Bourne

The Vets

Sixty pets in line,
Or is it sixty-nine?
Waiting for the vet,
And one of them is mine.

They all look very scared,
And none of them prepared.
Waiting for the vet,
At the door they glared.

'Come in,' the vet said
As I patted Monty's head.
He took him to a room
And laid him on the bed.

Monty was given a pill
Because he had been ill.
Now he wants to weigh him,
So I have to keep him still.

He'll be ok now I bet,
Now he has seen the vet.
He is my best friend
And the most lovable pet.

Victoria Roe (11)
The Robert Manning Technology College, Bourne

My First Day At School Haikus

My first day at school,
I was worried but happy,
The work is harder.

I got some homework,
All of the teachers are nice,
That was my first day.

Andrew Wand (11)
The Robert Manning Technology College, Bourne

Jack Sparrow

A tiny pink ball,
Sitting in our garden,
Shivering to death,
Was a tiny baby bird.

Dad brought him inside in his sweaty hands,
What were we to do?
Sitting under the warmth of the spotlight,
A bird of gloom.

We kept him for a night,
Maybe two, or maybe three,
Mum rang up the vet the next day,
But the news was not good.

We decided to keep him anyway,
The old hamster cage was his home,
We put in a perch or two,
His favourite sleeping place.

I was so glad I had him,
I treasured him like a child,
He made us laugh all of the time,
Our little baby, Jack Sparrow.

Jade Lane (11)
The Robert Manning Technology College, Bourne

Animals

A n animal can be,
N ice or sometimes you can see,
I t is going to be mean.
M ost people need to be keen,
A ll the time if they,
L ike to work with animals each day
S o, this shows animals are great.

Kerry Battams (11)
The Robert Manning Technology College, Bourne

Waves

Waves will crash
Under the sun
Waves will bash
Under the moon

Waves are cold
Waves are freezing
Waves are bold
Waves are pleasing

Waves fill up your heart with fear
From the liquid of the ocean
Waves make your eyes fill with a tear
From the waves in motion

Waves that leap and bound
In the endless sea
Are lost and never found

All these things fascinate me
All these things by the sea!

Daniel Morris (11)
The Robert Manning Technology College, Bourne

A Geography Poem

G eography teachers
E ncounter
'O rrible
G eography students
R ebelling
A gainst
P revalent
H omework
Y *awn!*

Jack Gandy (11)
The Robert Manning Technology College, Bourne

Football

The green grass,
The white ball,
The glowing fans,
The brilliant players,
Everyone enjoys it,
Most people play it,
All ages come together,
For this glorious game.

The green grass,
The white ball,
Win, lose or draw.
It doesn't matter about the score,
A nation brought together,
By this excellent game.

Tom Price (11)
The Robert Manning Technology College, Bourne

Weather

I like it when it's sunny,
So my bunny can hop about.

I don't like it when rain comes,
It becomes a pain.

I don't like it when it's windy,
Because you get blown away.

I like it when it snows,
Then you can have snow fights,
That's when the fun starts!

Aimee Hunt (11)
The Robert Manning Technology College, Bourne

What A Teacher Dreams

Have you ever wondered what a teacher dreams?
Let me tell you,
They dream of quiet children and no kids who are late,
Not even chairs that will scrape
No chewing gum, no chocolate and most of all
A teacher dreams of there being no more school!

Have you ever wondered what a teacher dreams?
Let me tell you,
They dream of no running in the corridors,
No wet playtimes and all thoughts, excuses and most of all
A teacher dreams of more summer holidays!

Karandeep Sahota (11)
The Robert Manning Technology College, Bourne

Rugby

Fifteen players make a team
All with one main theme
They're big, they're ugly and very mean
They are the rugby team.

They're wide, they're short, they're tall, they're fat
They don't use any bats
They use a ball, but it's not round
Most of the time they're on the ground.

Rugby, rugby, so much fun
But not when you're in the scrum
In the back is where it's best
Rugby is the greatest test.

Dominic Vidler-Green (11)
The Robert Manning Technology College, Bourne

A Hallowe'en Night

When the full moon rises,
Hallowe'en night is full of surprises.
Spookiness is in the air,
Black cats, voodoo dolls, all of it gives people a scare.
When people go out to 'trick or treat'
You never know who you might meet.
Ghosts, goblins and witches are around
They creep about without a sound.
Pumpkins frighten kids galore
But they still seem to come back for more.
Children dressing up for all to see
That's what Hallowe'en means to me.

Alice Penney (11)
The Robert Manning Technology College, Bourne

Beach Haikus

Listen to the beach.
The sound of waves is blissful.
Watching children play.

The sand is so smooth
Between my toes it tickles.
I do love beaches.

The sun is so strong.
It makes me feel so happy.
I do like beaches.

Beaches are nice at night.
The horizon is lovely.
Beaches are so nice.

Joshua Edwards (11)
The Robert Manning Technology College, Bourne

Poem About Midsummer Night's Dream

The people watching this play are very noisy and excited,
While the actors behind the curtain are getting very nervous,
At the thought of acting in front of loads of people,
Thinking it will go terribly wrong, but when it's time to get on stage
Their nerves begin to stop.

When they start to speak, everyone is watching
They begin laughing at the jokes they're saying,
They sing and dance and make everyone laugh till the end
                                        of the play.

At the end of the play, behind the curtain
Bottom has something to say,
'It feels like we have just begun
When suddenly it's over
I have now decided to do another play in Dover
Because I really enjoyed the one we just did.'

Stephanie Gostling (12)
The Robert Manning Technology College, Bourne

Autumn Poem

He wanders through night and day,
Leaves shrivelling as he passes.
Summer flowers dying everywhere,
Angry gardeners having to clear up.
He flows through towns, cities and countries,
Working with wind and rain,
Causes trains to be delayed and people to be late for work.
He has his fun.
But now is done.
As Winter chases him out!

George Hughes (11)
The Robert Manning Technology College, Bourne

Floridian Holiday

Big holidays come once a year with my family and I,
Off to shores afar we go to the airport to fly up high.
Florida is my favourite place to go with Universal, Epcot and MGM.
We go on the roller coasters, round and round we go,
With screams of excitement and our faces all aglow.
Then home to our villa with its air conditioning and pool,
Where I can swim and chill, before going to Disney to shout
like a fool.
It would be great to live life as one big holiday
But I know soon it will be over and back to England for a school day.

David Jackson (11)
The Robert Manning Technology College, Bourne

Fireworks

Fireworks dancing in the night
Jumping around exploding with light
People on the ground seeing this spectacular sight
In all its glory and might
As they take flight screaming and whistling into the night
Magical colours fill the sky
Then disappear to die.

James Mason (12)
The Robert Manning Technology College, Bourne

My Big Sister!

Kirsty is my big sister, she really is a pain!
Whenever she is naughty, I always take the blame
She takes all my jewellery and make-up
And when the alarm rings in the morning
She shouts at and screams because I won't wake up.
Kirsty is my sister, she really is a pain!

Elizabeth Manning (11)
The Robert Manning Technology College, Bourne

Seasons

In winter it is cold and chilly,
That makes us want to wrap up,
Nearly all of us have colds, and others do not,
If we went to the woods,
We would see the flowers and trees are covered in snow.

In spring all the flowers are growing,
And the trees are looking more pretty,
It's still a bit cold, but it is sunny
It is just the way it should be,
It is not too cold, not too warm, it is just right.

In autumn I am very sorry to say
That the beautiful leaves are falling,
It is time when it falls off,
So later it can grow even more pretty
It will soon grow back to normal.

In summer I am very glad, at last it is hot,
I know what I will be doing
Going down to the warmth of the beach,
It will make you happy.

Lidia Dodsworth (11)
The Robert Manning Technology College, Bourne

Football

F ootball is great
O h, what a goal!
O ther players watch out
T op corner
B ottom corner
A ll the crowd went wild
L ob the keeper
L ove the sport.

Richard Powell (11)
The Robert Manning Technology College, Bourne

Deadly Winds

The tornado is like a cheetah
It destroys things like a wild animal.

The tornado looks scary in the face,
It's a dangerous thing, because it destroys.

It hides, then it pounces on its prey,
It kills people and animals with its sharp teeth.

Deadly and slyly it weaves in and out.
Like a deadly cheetah in the bush.

Mark Goff (11)
Trinity House School, Hull

Cheetah Roar

It looks like a cheetah eating things up.
It leaves all the heavy and hard things alone.
It rips up houses like a cheetah with prey.

It chases things until it catches them,
And eats it to the bone.
It smells of the things it gobbles up.

It sounds loud like a cheetah's roar,
It twirls like baby cheetahs playing with butterflies.

Jack Barker (11)
Trinity House School, Hull

The Wind, The Weather, The Waves

The wind is like water,
Swishing down a whale's mouth.

The waves are like big rolling toilet tubes,
Crashing into the rocks with anger.

The waves sound like a lion roaring through a microphone,
The waves smell like salty bacon with seaweed.

Harvey Cosway (11)
Trinity House School, Hull

The Tornado Elephant

The elephant's actions are like a tornado crashing into houses,
Like a bowling ball hitting pins.
The strong elephant throws its victims around with its great tusks.
Just like a tornado throwing out bodies.

The breath of the elephant smells like rubbish waiting to be
cleared away.
The feet of the elephant are as big as cars,
When it stands on cars it makes a crashing noise like
glass smashing.

The elephant runs into the park confused, it begins to run.
Killing people in its path, throwing trees about, people scream,
But then it dies and it's quiet, quiet, quiet.

Lewis Burns (11)
Trinity House School, Hull

Twist

Fast and thin it likes to spin.
As fast as Concorde, it whips around.
It has a mouth so big it can bring anything in.
It's fast and it likes to twist.

Red-hot with fury, it charges
The whistling you hear at night, you will know it is charging.
Then it twists and sucks
It's fast and it likes to twist.

Destruction is what it causes
Eyes like looking knives,
Kills anything and anyone
It's fast and it likes to twist.

Alex McCoy (11)
Trinity House School, Hull

Prowling Thunderstorm

You only see him for a split second as he pounces,
His contrasting coat flashes in your eyes,
Roaring thunder, dark as the cheetah's mouth,
It's a raging ball of fur.

Its breath stinks like an old rotting kipper when sunny and hot,
The roar thunders miles away,
In another world even,
But you'll always remember it was there.

You'll never forget that it was there,
It leaves you homeless,
It leaves you supplyless,
It leaves you without hope.

Aiden Andrews-McDermott (11)
Trinity House School, Hull

The Roaring Sea

Like a tiger roaring, banging, snapping waves
Cheering on their best teammates
As they're snapping, roaring, banging
All their mates are still tanning.

As the match carries on
The two waves are planning on
As they start to calm down
One of the waves eased his frown.

As the bells on his collar finally ring
The two waves began
To sing with a
Roar!

Billy Kinnersley (11)
Trinity House School, Hull

Spinning

The hurricane is brown like Taz
Looking angry and vicious
With its big teeth spinning away rapidly
Messy, ruffled-up hair.

Sounds like a lawnmower
And a tractor engine.
Smells like the sewer
Mixed together with slurry.

It hunts down anything in its path then eats it
Keeping every race down.
Gets out of control,
Violently assaulting things,
Moving long distances at a time.

Patrick Sheriff (12)
Trinity House School, Hull

My Poem

The gigantic mountain topped with snow,
A place where many dare not to go,
To climb up high, may take your breath,
But be careful you don't fall to your death.

The ice-cold touch,
Of a white mountain,
And the fresh smell,
Is like a fully grown fountain.

The snow starts to melt,
To form into a river,
It's freezing cold,
I start to shiver.

Ryan Lamb (11)
Trinity House School, Hull

The Rhino

The tornado is a rhino,
The rhino is tough as rocks,
The rhino's face is a T-Rex
It is really scary.

The rhino smells of smoke, like the smoke from the fires
The tornado causes by blowing things up.
Its breath smells like a bin of rotten maggots,
The rhino sounds like thunder, it can hear things miles away.

The tornado is destruction, a killing machine like the rhino,
The rhino hits things like a football hitting the net,
The tornado destroys people's houses and leaves them homeless,
The rhino disappears like a tornado dying away.

Jamie Walters (11)
Trinity House School, Hull

Snow Dove

The snow falls quietly from the grey skies,
Smooth and silent as when a dove flies,
Dancing white feathers fly fast and gracefully,
The blizzard blows hard ice and glacially.

The crunch of the snow, the ice-cold smell,
Dull is the sound of this cotton wool shell,
The dove pecks for food to take to its nest,
Its quiet cooing calls from its snow-white chest.

The blizzard lays its feathery bed,
The world is covered as the sun rears its head
Quietly the wind slows and dies,
Grey clouds clear to reveal blue skies.

Lewis Brady (11)
Trinity House School, Hull

The Comparison Of A Wolf To Snowy Mountains

The mountain is in its white coat like a wolf
When the snow came, it roamed as it pleased
Landing on the rocky surface
And soon it will roam again.

The roaming is popular, the resting is rare.
With the edgy and jagged mountain like it's past its home
Even the regular roaming is sometimes without heart.

It camouflages like a lettuce in a forest
As it pleases it can go,
As fast as a Formula 1 car
And as slow as a snail.

Daniel Barker (11)
Trinity House School, Hull

The Morning Sea

The sea starts to mime whilst making a rhyme,
The waves are really calm like a snail eating a lime
It moves as if it is an injured snail
Walking in hours' time.

The sea smells salty
A snail is bolty
If the snail goes in the sea it will start to die
So then it's time to say goodbye.

The sea and snail lounge around like a drunk, lazy man
Drinking out of a can
The snail gets blown away because it is so still.
So still, so still, so still, so still.

Richard Appleton (11)
Trinity House School, Hull

Lizard-Blizzard

Racing through the brown and white town,
Blizzard dashing round and round.
Pounding at the small villages,
As the mountain weather rages.

The blizzard is an enraged lizard,
Scraping up the soft white snow.
Its shredded skin blows gradually down,
Its breath fills the air like icy wind.

Pounces on people and knocks them down
Its cold-blooded body fills the town.
The lizard starts to retreat to the woods,
But it will return, it will reap.

Ross Williamson (11)
Trinity House School, Hull

The Polar Bear

The snow is as white as a polar bear,
Standing out like a ghost in a haunted house.

The snow approaches the ground, like a polar bear
Approaching its prey, so slow, so quiet.

It covers the ground in a thick white quilt,
Like the polar bear roaming the land as it is king.

Then the sun comes out and melts the snow,
Like the hunters murdering the polar bears with their shotguns,
And then it happens all over again a year later.

Ashley Rogers (11)
Trinity House School, Hull

The Yeti Attack

There is a mountain like a huge yeti,
This yeti is extremely tall
If you were to see it, you'd say I'm having a laugh
Because up to his chest, he has had a mud bath.

What a disgusting smell it does have
However, sometimes it's very fresh
You'd be able to smell, that urine smell,
Even if you had a blocked nose.

Outrageously, it spits up fire, lava and rocks
This guy thinks he owns the world,
However, sometimes he freezes people to his peak.
Now it is time to go to bed and have a good night's sleep!

Oliver Collins (11)
Trinity House School, Hull

The Bear

The bear raged around the wood
Like the heat spreading around the Earth.
Its eyes tightened up
As though as it was just about to pounce on its prey.
His breath smelt
As though he'd been eating rotting maggots from the floor,
As he plodded around the mountain searching for his supper.
There's not many of them left on the mountain.
One by one they go, hunters, searching for them.
It's too hot for them to get water.
Heat takes its toll.

Joe Gay (11)
Trinity House School, Hull

My Poem

The volcano is like the Tasmanian devil,
It sits quietly, calmly and still, and suddenly explodes into anger
Ripping and burning whatever comes in its path.

Its breath is like hot ash burning in the wind.
Its angry mouth sounds terrifying
As if it was a whole rugby stadium which is jam-packed.

Its nasty look looks as ugly as a pig rolling in maggots,
And when it speaks,
Hot fire explodes out of the ferocious beast's wide open mouth.

Michael Pearson (11)
Trinity House School, Hull

Weather Poem

The lion's eyes are as big as two moons.
His hair is as bright as the sun's shine.
The lion is as fast as the lava flowing down the side.

As the lion roars it sounds like a huge volcano erupting.
He smells like a bin, forgotten to be cleaned.

The lion's mouth is like a crushing machine as it speeds for its prey.
It is like lava flowing down the side.

Sultan Idmisov (11)
Trinity House School, Hull

Earthquake

The earthquake is like a snake slithering along the ground,
Dropping rocks while it crawls.

The earthquake scares people as it crawls, terrifying people
Nearly making their skeletons jump out of their skin.

The earthquake is like a snake slithering, like a bull in a china shop,
Like a nuclear bomb about to hit the Earth.

Reece Woods (11)
Trinity House School, Hull

The Galloping Sea

The sea is a giant white horse with a fine white coat
Which blends with the colour of the sea's foam,
And has feet of solid rock which pound the seabed.

The horse smells strong, as strong as the salt in the air,
And sounds like a jet flying over the sea, heading towards base,
Like the horse going to shore.

It powers itself to shore, galloping with a great force,
Jumping over obstacles in its way.
Until it finally reaches shore and curls over to rest.

Ryan Barr (11)
Trinity House School, Hull

Untitled

As I walk through the school gates
I go up and chat to all my mates
I say, 'Where's John?' but nobody knows
I say, 'Let's walk,' but the school bell goes.

In the first lesson, maths that day
The teacher says to me, 'Learn don't play!'
I get a bit angry and my face goes red
I wish I was at home asleep in my bed.

The bell goes again - break time it is
I go to the tuck shop and speak to my friend Liz
I buy some toast and a milkshake too
I spend some of my money as I do up my shoe.

It's the last period, tech that day
I get a metal saw and I saw away
It's quarter-past-three and we all pack away
The bell goes again and we go home, *'Hurray!'*

Thomas Hooton (13)
Vale of Ancholme Technology College, Brigg

Ode To A Penguin

Observe the majestic penguin in its natural habitat,
The way it catches fish,
The way no human can
Then it eats a cheese flan and has a sausage pie.

Observe the majestic penguin as it builds a cosy nest,
Amongst the freezing snow,
Where no human can survive,
Then it has a tea party with a tortoise.

Observe the majestic penguin,
The bird that cannot fly,
It surely proves that birds don't need to,
Then it sneezes on a cheeseburger.

Observe the majestic penguin as it eats its captured prey,
It dives down to find some fish,
It will eat them for breakfast,
With chips and tomato ketchup.

Observe the majestic penguin as it escapes the killer whale,
It then swims back to the beach,
Where it is safe,
Then it plays chequers with a duck.

Josh Shaw (12)
Vale of Ancholme Technology College, Brigg

Feet

They come in all shapes and sizes,
Small, long, fat, thin.
They also come in two aromas,
Minty fresh and cheesy cravings.
Oh well, at least it was the truth!

Aimee-Lauren Westwood (12)
Vale of Ancholme Technology College, Brigg

Drugs

Drugs are sad,
And are really, really bad.

Don't take any drug,
If you do you're probably a mug.

They ruin lives,
And make you use knives.

Don't be dealing,
Because you might start stealing.

Don't give in to crime,
Because in your life you don't have much time.

You'll end up in jail,
And you'll always hear a wail.

It really is hell,
And someone will tell.

You should always remember this,
Because otherwise you'll have no bliss.

James Clark (12)
Vale of Ancholme Technology College, Brigg

Bullying

Unless you have a reason, don't do it
Let someone know what is happening to you
Let someone help you
You should get help from people you can trust
In the end the facts come out
Never show you are scared
Get help as soon as you can.

Richard Smelt (12)
Vale of Ancholme Technology College, Brigg

Interests

Fencing is interesting,
Clashes sword to sword,
When I go to fencing,
I am never ever bored!

Penguins are funny,
Sliding here and there,
Penguins eat fishes,
And they are everywhere!

Both these are my interests,
I like these very much,
But I like best my teddy bear,
With which I hug and clutch!

Jake Beasley (13)
Vale of Ancholme Technology College, Brigg

The Shark

Be aware
For the dangerous stare
If you look them in the eye
For this could be
The last thing you see
Just before you die.

Their mighty snap will
Break your back
With all your might
You could put up a fight
But still it would do no good.

Daniel Smith (12)
Vale of Ancholme Technology College, Brigg

Who Are You?

Here I stand in the world today,
The world's still fighting like yesterday,
What have they done?
We don't know,
But we follow the crowd,
Wherever they go.

They lie about things,
To get their own way,
People will kill children,
Nearly every day,
Listen to us,
But you just won't,
We are the people,
Wherever we go.

What's the point of writing this?
Nobody will listen,
This is hurting your people
What have we done?
We don't know,
But we follow the crowd,
Wherever they go.

We are the people,
So let us choose,
We know what we want to do,
But yet you make the decisions
Of what we do,
Who are you?
And what do you do?

Adelle Grierson (14)
Vale of Ancholme Technology College, Brigg

Feelings!

I walk round the streets
With my friends
I think, *is this what I'm living for?*
Then he walks past
And smiles
I get shivers
As I smell his deodorant
As I did when I had him in my arms
Only the other week
I go depressed
Down to my knees
I go
Back to step one
With no one to love
And no one to care for.

Amy Thompson (13)
Vale of Ancholme Technology College, Brigg

The Wonders Of Christmas

In the winter when the snow falls
Jack Frost comes to call
He decorates the world with a blanket of ice
Wrap up warm, all cosy and nice.

The animals hibernate in their little beds
Goodnight little sleepy heads
Santa Claus is nearly here
With all his reindeer, let's give a big cheer.

Children sleep, while Santa creeps
Santa eats his Christmas treats
He lays the presents under the tree
For all the little children to see!

Jade Ronald & Charlotte Robinson (13)
Vale of Ancholme Technology College, Brigg

I Really Want That!

I really want a dog,
Or maybe even a frog,
I can't have a cat,
'Cos I'm allergic to that.

I've already had a fish - but they are such a bore,
I only want to make four,
I've already had three,
So, just one more - see.

So I stick with my teddy bears,
It's so unfair!
Stuffed animals can't move or run,
Plus, they're no fun!

Rebecca Cheong (12)
Vale of Ancholme Technology College, Brigg

Love

Love is stronger than life,
Like a beautiful butterfly, it
Struggles but will never die,
Love is like a rose
It blooms so often,
And lets out its scent of love,
To love and to be loved,
It's like an extraordinary
Gift from the gods, but
Love is nothing,
Without freedom or truth,
Love is a feeling from the heart
That will always survive.

Alicia Rhodes (12)
Vale of Ancholme Technology College, Brigg

Boys V Girls

Boys are cute
Girls play the flute
Boys are fit
Girls do the splits.

Boys play ball
Girls go to the mall
Boys ride bikes
Girls sing in mics.

Boys are a mess
Girls like to dress
Boys descended from apes
Girls come from beautiful grapes.

After all the hate
Why do we date?

Jasmine Richardson & Lauren Russell (11)
Vale of Ancholme Technology College, Brigg

The Tortoise

The tortoise's claws are round and sharp,
They grip the ground, and let the tortoise move surely and steadily.

The tortoise's legs are scaly and powerful,
Slowly plodding to its destination.

The tortoise's shell is impenetrable even to a lion,
It is patterned like a mosaic, a fine work of art.

The tortoise's head is like a small snake,
Retreating into its shell when danger comes.

The tortoise's eye is shiny like a black pearl,
Always focusing on a brighter future.

Tim Metcalfe (12)
Vale of Ancholme Technology College, Brigg